DON'T PLANT PEAS AND EXPECT SPAGHETTI

A CoffeeTime Collection

Andy & Renie Bowman

Praise for Andy & Renie Bowman

"Good, clean, down-home country humor, wisdom, and just plain common sense seems to be fading away here in America, as the Woke culture war continues. In their book, Renie and Andy Bowman confront all of that, and more. This book is a good read that will give you a chuckle. Plus, it will make you think, and cause you to appreciate our country. And the awesome God we serve. This book will brighten up your day. You will enjoy...no...definitely enjoy this book!"

Jimmy Houston, Professional Angler, TV personality, B.A.S.S Hall of Fame; Oklahoma Sports Hall Of Fame

"Coffee Time with Andy and Renie Bowman inspires their listeners and readers to deal with real life situations in a way that pleases the Lord. I am very pleased to recommend this book that can serve as a daily devotion that offers a positive outlook on life's challenges."

Randall Christy, The Gospel Station Network; Executive Director of The Great Passion Play, Eureka Springs AR

"Coffeetime Column" is the most popular column in our three newspaper publications. It is filled with wit and wisdom. We have encouraged Andy and Renie to publish a book for a long time and are so thankful they have decided to do so. It will be a blessing to so many people, and we can't wait to order our copy!"

Bill & Dayna Robinson, Owners and publishers; Holdenville Tribune, Holdenville, Okla; Allen Advocate, Allen, Okla; Coalgate Record Register, Coalgate, Okla

"What a delightful compilation of straight-from-the-heart homespun wisdom, encouragement, humor, and insight! Always engaging, the articles speak to everyday issues with a mix of common sense and Christian truth. You will smile, laugh, wipe a tear, and often want to shout "Amen!"

Dr. Anthony Jordan, Executive Director, Oklahoma Baptist General Convention, Retired

"Renie and Andy just have that 'home spun' way of expressing biblical truth creatively! I highly recommend their humorous stories (some of them may be true) to help transform and challenge you with every turn of the page!"

Dr. Kent Choate, MAMFC, Ph.D., Pastoral Counselor, Sapulpa, Oklahoma

"During the present time, it appears everything in our lives is being driven by hate, who's right, who's wrong, politics, and social media. As a publisher, I have vowed to keep the Bible a part of my newspaper. CoffeeTime Column was perfect for our community. Renie and Andy Bowman take a verse and give it current life meaning. We all have to do our part to drown out the negative and keep God present. They do just that with their column."

Maurisa Nelson, Publisher and Editor; Ada News, Ada, Okla.

"I can gladly endorse this work by Renie & Andy Bowman, you will not be disappointed."

Jeremy McCaslin, Publisher; The Good Life of Broken Arrow Magazine, Broken Arrow, Okla.

This book is dedicated to our close friend and sister-in-faith, Linda Jones.

You harassed us for two years, asking us to make our
CoffeeTime Columns into a book.

Well, Sis, we finally listened, and here is the outcome.
Thanks for being persistent.

Copyright © 2022 by Andy & Renie Bowman

All rights reserved. No part of this book may be reproduced or used in any
manner without written permission of the copyright owner except for the use
of quotations in a book review.

First paperback edition October 2022

Book design by Valley Way Media
Cover and author photos by Jill Solomon Wise
Interior photos courtesy of pixabay.com and motionarray.com

ISBN 979-8-218-08260-4 (paperback)

www.coffeetimecolumn.com

CONTENTS

ACKNOWLEDGEMENTS	vii
INTRODUCTION	ix

I - LIVING: NOT FOR THE FAINT-HEARTED — 1
Gotta Learn When to Let Go of the Rope	3
Coffee Cups Have Rims for a Reason	5
The Runaway	7
Being Whetstoned? You Better Believe it Hurts	9
Better Get a Deep Seat and a Tight Hold	11
Coddling is a Killer	13
Free Belly Laughs	15
I Can't Find It	18
Goofballs, Bullies and All the Rest of Us	20
Boundaries are Meant to Bring About Necessary Pain	22

II - PRIDE, PREJUDICE AND OTHER PROBLEMS WITH US — 25
Run That Fool Mule!	27
Instruction Manual? Nah, Don't Need It.	29
Is She the Only Living Person in the Room?	31
Bullybirds	33
I Don't Need Help, I Got This	35
I Shore 'Nuff Hate It When the Wife Gets Sick	37
Disasterous Dog-Dipping Days	39

III - MARRIAGE AND THUNDERSTORMS: BOTH FROM HEAVEN — 43
Don't Do That If it Hurts	45
Are Men Really Just That Blind	47
The Counsellor Grabbed Her and Kissed Her	49
Marriage Can Be Like Coffee and Creamer	51
Song and Dance on the Battlefield	53
Beware of Forcing Your Mate to Compete	55
It All Starts With a Stand-Off	57
A Five-Hour Feast Yesterday is No Good Today	60

IV - CHOICES: YOU HAVE TO LIVE WITH THEM — 63
Wheat Jeans, a Girl, and Johnson Grass	65
The Bed was Already on Fire	67
Fences and Stupid Cows	69
Constantly Reliving the Pain Won't Change the Past	71
It's Just What Snakes Do	73
The King's Fool	75

They... Almost... Won the Game	77
Stupid Expects Change- But With No Changes	79

V - KIDS: YOU SAID YOU WANTED THEM — 83

Beware: Hellion Alert	85
One Mo' Time!	87
Kids Love the Trash	89
Are the Baby Cradles Rocked Anymore?	91
Fail or Succeed, But Let Them Choose Their Path	93
Don't Leave Your Kids the Legacy of Limping	95
Tiny Tyrant Never Been Spanked- and it Shows	97
Christmastime With Dad	99

VI - BECOMING A GROWNUP: GRIT YOUR TEETH AND BEAR IT — 103

Things Are Not Always As They Appear	105
Own It... It's Yours	107
Look at That One With the Limp and the Bandage	109
Hammers, Pigs and Cows Can Make a Farmer Cuss	111
If It's Already Bad News, Don't Make It Worse	113
A Bleeding Bottom Lip is Better Than Smelling Skunky	115
See & Be- That Is A Lie	117
Now Understand, I'm Just Tellin' You What I Heard	119
Don't Plant Peas and Expect Spaghetti	121
Churchese is a Foreign Language	123

VII - INTEGRITY: IT AIN'T ALWAYS EASY — 127

Stand Your Ground, Sweet Lady	129
No Lawyers or Courts Needed on Their Land	131
Better Check Your Fly, Preacher!	133
B.O.L.O. For These People	135
Facebook Shouldn'y Be a Dirty Laundry Bin	137
A Huge Salute to All The Caretakers Out There	139
Looking For a Huge Dumpster	142
If Nothing Else, Salute The Uniform	144

VIII - WE'RE ALL A MESS, BUT GOD'S FIXING THAT — 147

But... Please Doc, Not My Coffee!	149
Does the Almighty Creator Ever Make Mistakes?	151
Who Are You Rooting For?	153
Pappa Only Wanted The Best For Her	155
Drink, People, Drink!	157
Father Isn't Necessarily Spelled F-A-T-H-E-R	159
God Isn't Trying to Spoil Your Fun	161
The Mild-Mannered and The Revenge Seeker	163
Stinkin' Thinkin'	165
You Can Be a Different You	167

CONCLUSION — 171

ACKNOWLEDGEMENTS

We are so thankful that our Lord Jesus Christ brought these people into our lives. They have helped to make our ministry and this book possible.

Jill Solomon Wise – more than our photographer and friend, you opened our eyes to the possibilities of life after retirement.

Ben Beresh – we couldn't have done this without your encouragement, tech expertise and your guidance.

Dr. Jessie Miller – The chiropractor who keeps our bones together and headed in the same direction. Physically, we couldn't stay doing what we do every day, without you.

Dr. Bill Tims – World's best nutritionist in our eyes. Longtime guide and friend, we owe our ongoing good health to you.

The McCurtain Gazette, Idabel, Ok – you gave the kickstart to a whole new career.

Our family, friends and supporters – you've read, listened, critiqued, encouraged, and laughed with us - through it all.

INTRODUCTION

While pastoring in S. E. Oklahoma, Andy was asked to write a column for the local newspaper. He was to temporarily fill in for the regular writer, a local minister struggling with serious illness. When Rev. Bobby Ashley passed away, the newspaper asked Andy to continue contributing his weekly article. So was the beginning of "CoffeeTime Column With Brother Andy."

Renie had critiqued, contributed and edited her husband's column for several years, but it soon became evident that while Andy was a veteran public speaker and preacher, she was the one who truly loved writing. So, the CoffeeTime Column went through a "re-birth" to emerge as "CoffeeTime With Andy & Renie," with Renie as the principal writer, and Andy as the idea guy and collaborator.

Years passed, then the time came when Andy needed to retire from pastoring, due to medical issues. So, they moved to Broken Arrow, Oklahoma but continued to write for that first paper. That was interesting and good, but soon Andy had bigger ideas. To date, that weekly column is in over one hundred twenty-five newspapers and magazines across the country. And increasing in number as quickly as Andy can contact editors and then convince Renie to send out sample packets to them.

In 2022, the first CoffeeTime With Andy & Renie Podcast went online on their website. They also have a radio slot by the same name, that can be found three times every day on any of the twenty stations of The Gospel Station Network. In addition to these ministries, they continue singing, preaching and speaking in every venue they can.

Writing this book is the next segment of their journey with God. Who knows what path He will put them on in the future? That, dear friends, is part of the adventure!

I

LIVING:
NOT FOR THE FAINT-HEARTED

GOTTA LEARN WHEN TO LET GO OF THE ROPE

Two young boys were growing up on their parents' small farm. This meant that raising show-worthy pigs and calves for livestock shows was a normal thing in life to them.

Bobby, the youngest of the two, was small in stature and big in heart. That year he had spent his hard-earned money for a quality steer that he carefully groomed every day, readying it for the shows. Daily he faithfully fed, watered and brushed it. Eventually his dad put a halter on the steer, so that its lead training could begin.

There was only one problem. Aptly named, Crazy Charlie hated being told where to go and what to do. Kicking and bellowing, Charley resisted any attempt to gentle him, let alone teach him to follow directions in the show ring. The problem was bad enough that dad had given strict instructions to the boy that he was never to attempt to train him all alone.

You did read the earlier reference to small in stature and big in heart?

One day while dad was away from the farm, the determined and energetic twelve-year-old decided that it was time to try to handle Crazy Charley on his own. Slipping away from his older brother, he walked to the corral where his nemesis was peacefully hanging out. Glittering daydreams were in his head of his dad coming home that evening to a calm Charley walking peacefully beside him. Gazing adoringly at his master and following his every command.

Taking a lead rope from the barn, he carefully approached the now suspicious Charley. Successfully attaching the lead rope to the halter, he led the wild-eyed steer out of the corral and through the gate into a much larger pen. But the millisecond the gate swung open all Hell broke loose in the form of a Crazy-Charley-On-Triple-Steroids.

From inside the house, the older brother heard terrified calf bellows and even louder human profanities coming from the pen. Sprinting toward the barn, he could see Crazy Charley racing at full tilt, shrieking his head off while dragging sixty-pound little Bobby at the end of the rope. Said brother had been jerked off his feet and was now bouncing headlong behind that scared seven-hundred-pound animal. Hanging on for dear life, every breath the boy took he was using to scream angry obscenities at the calf, which only caused it to panic and run harder.

The older brother started yelling at the top of his lungs, trying to get Bouncing Bobby to "Let go! Turn loose of the @%*# rope!" But he stubbornly refused, so Bobby and Crazy Charley made another couple of rounds around the pen, before it all ended in a cloud of dust when the calf finally swung him into the surrounding barbed wire fence.

Now, folks, commitment is a good thing. But stupidity? That's a whole 'nuther ball game. Gotta learn when to let go of the rope.

COFFEE CUPS HAVE RIMS FOR A REASON

I quickly poured my cup of coffee as soon as it was hot and ready. Had been looking forward to it all the way to the office that morning. Well, yes, I could have been a little too eager. And I guess I may have been a little distracted. Thankfully I looked down the millisecond before my full cup ran all over the countertop. Another spoonful of coffee and I would have been cleaning.

But it still all looked just fine. After all, full is good. Really, no problem. I might have to be a little more careful than normal as I carry it to my desk. But hey, c'mon, I do have average motor skills. Surely I can carry a full cup of coffee across a room.

But after a few cautious steps it happened. In the middle of a balancing act worthy of the Flying Wallendas, a little of the coffee sloshed over the top of the cup and onto my hand. The instant pain caused me to instinctively jerk…no need to say any more, you know what happened. Now I had a stinging hand, a mess to clean up, and a definitely darker outlook on my morning. All because I put too much coffee in my cup and I exceeded its limits.

Reminds me of a lot of well-meaning folks today. They plan and schedule and cram so many things into their twenty-nine-hour-days that they can't really handle any of it well. Not for very long, anyway. Folks, remember, we humans do have limits. Squeezing spouse, family, work, play, church time, and community obligations into our lives is hard. It doesn't matter how great your juggling skills, your balancing ability, or your coping skills – you have a limit.

Everyone has a rim on their personal 'coffee cup' that warns them enough is enough. And if it is ignored, there will come a time when scalding hot coffee runs over the top. The pain that results will cause a reaction that can be felt by everyone who touches your life. It may be an explosion or could be a slow meltdown. Regardless of how it happens, a certain amount of mess is the result.

A coffee cup can only hold just so much, and then the cupbearer feels the result.

Good lesson. Effective learning tool. Smarter person.

THE RUNAWAY

Needing play-around money, as all young teenagers do, years ago three industrious farm boys decided to earn some cash by creating their own hay-hauling crew one summer. So they made a plan. One boy would drive as another loaded the hay, while the third teen would stack it onto their borrowed truck.

Very important that you note the 'borrowed.'

All worked well until the fateful cloudy day when they ran into a huge problem. One of those enterprising young men simply didn't show up. Now if you are not aware, hay left waiting in the field on a day threatening rain is not too accommodating. And the owner of said field even less. Owners do not appreciate hay not stacked in a dry barn. Rain can cause it to be molded by moisture. And that ruined mess costs the owner an enormous amount of money. Leaving hay-haulers to face a very furious farmer.

So that morning, the two boys were standing in the field checking their watches, eyeing the thickening clouds, slapping their work gloves on the fence, and kicking dirt clods in frustration. Finally, they realized their friend was simply not going to show up, and they had no choice but to get creative.

So, after giving their problem some brain-time, they decided to try replacing Absent Aaron with a rock balanced strategically on the gas pedal. Freeing them to load and stack. Absolute genius!

They eventually found the perfect rock, and after adjusting it just so-so, they threw the truck in low gear and began working. When they came to the end of a row, one would jump in and turn the truck around. They loaded and stacked this way all day, and the whole procedure was working perfectly.

Until.

At the end of the day, they came upon a portion of the field where the ground was a little unlevel. A lot unlevel. And their borrowed truck, now rigged up to be their fancy automated hay truck, ran over a deep dip. Causing the rock that had been sitting so meekly in its assigned place to decide it was time to shift its weight forward on the gas pedal.

The two exhausted boys suddenly found themselves screaming obscenities, throwing gloves and chasing after a runaway. After a frantic chase, one boy finally caught up to the truck, climbed in and stomped on the brakes - less than fifty feet from a large pond. (Did I forget to mention the truck owner had said that any damages would be on their head?)

Sounds perzactly like life for you and me, if we have the guts to admit it to anybody.

We hit a problem, and we eventually find a way to fix it. Indeed, we almost break an arm patting ourself on the back, congratulating ourself for our cleverness. All goes well until the stupid rock shifts, and life goes into hyperdrive – headed directly for a pond. If we are fast enough, we avoid a dunking. If not, then we have to learn to swim...very quickly.

But always remember, folks, as long you are breathing you do have a chance to chase your runaway. Don't simply let your life race headlong into a pond. Chase it down and fix it, for as long as you possibly can.

BEING WHETSTONED? YOU BETTER BELIEVE IT HURTS

Ever used a dull steak knife and had to hack and tear your way thru a rib eye? Ever tried to use a pair of scissors that lost its sharp edge a long time ago? Both utensils are ineffective at best, and can actually mutilate what you are trying to do. A device due for a date with a whetstone can frustrate the be-jeebers out of you.

Andy's grandad knew that a rough whetstone applied to a dull blade makes a sharp usable tool. But he also knew there was an art to using that whetstone. The art; patience while applying that stone at the correct angle to the blade. No untrained dude can haphazardly run the blade along that whetstone and expect a perfectly sharpened edge. An ignorant whetstone user can actually do more harm than good.

Why does a whetstone work? The rough and gritty surface applied over and over to a blade grinds away the pocks and imperfections on the edge of that blade – eventually producing a sharp edge that is useful.

But did I mention it takes time and repeated effort? "Quick and easy going" doesn't cut it when using a whetstone. (Oh yeah, pun definitely intended.) And having to use patience? A razor-like edge can only be accomplished by sharpening both sides of the blade. Yep, ya gotta turn around and do to the other side what you just did to the first side. Like I said…patience.

Now, use your imagination with me.

Who is the dull blade that is placed in the hands of a Master Whetstoner, the one who works patiently to make it useful and sharp? You and me, of course. (Surely, we are not so dull as to not recognize that fact.)

And Who is the one holding His badly pocked blade in one hand and the whetstone in the other? Our Creator and our God.

And the whetstone that scrapes away at that dull blade until it is sharp and effective in His hand? Life.

Dealing with life's daily victories and heartaches has a way of giving us problems. One of those problems is our pride. We can start to believe we have learned all there is and now we are totally mature - sharp and useful. Seeing ourselves as God's gift to the world. Until God steps in with His whetstone and begins to work on our weaknesses. That's the part that stings. Then He turns us around and starts in on the other side!

Fun…not so much. Needed…absolutely. Inevitable…as sure as the earth spinning on its axis. Time-consuming…as long as we live on this earth.

Lessons from the whetstone… You are not perfect. But you are in the hands of the Perfect One who is applying life to get you closer to that point. And it is all for His purposes. He is patient and skillful at what He is doing.

Sure, it hurts sometimes. And it's going to take your entire life. Because we tend to be a tad stubborn, and the Master Whetstoner never gives up. He accepts you just as you are. But at the same time, He's determined you will be an even better you - after His whetstone has been skillfully applied.

BETTER GET A DEEP SEAT AND A TIGHT HOLD

The first month of 2020 gave no indication just how rough the ride was going to be for everyone in the USA for the next few years. Our big ol' country had fairly-run-of-the-mill problems and successes the first couple of months. Little did we innocents suspect what was just around the corner - come March. But it didn't take long for us to become a whole bunch wiser.

Because of what we have been through, "Get a deep seat and a tight hold" is a rodeo phrase that even the most confirmed city-bred folks now understand. And we really don't have an idea what this wild horse called "Life" may try next. Not only does this bucking bronco show no sign of running out of steam, it seems to be getting its second wind. It's already thrown us out of the saddle and flat on our derriere several times with COVID-19. Twisted us in a tight spiral with a traumatic Presidential election. And we still have to deal with our beloved weather throwing tantrums at the drop of a hat. It has always had the ability to toss our country into the air and then kick us in the gut when we land on the ground.

Reminds me of the story a young man named Terry told us a few years ago. Seems he grew up on the farm around horses, so he developed a love for those beautiful, strong animals. One day when he was a young boy, his dad came home with a gorgeous black horse named Joe and told the boy that it was his, "When you break him to ride."

"No problem. After all, I'm almost eleven years old and nearly grown," Terry thought confidently. "I can get him eating out of my hand in no time flat."

Terry spent time making friends with Joe. Good-natured and calm, the horse was a sweetheart. Finally, the big day arrived and his dad helped the excited boy saddle up. Joe remained cool as a cucumber through that process. Then he stood with quiet patience as dad helped Terry swing into the saddle for the very first time. But after helping him adjust the reins in his small hands, Terry's dad looked him in the eye and warned, "Better get a deep seat and a tight hold, 'cause it's likely to get a little bit rough."

'Yeah sure, no problem,' blind optimism said, 'I got this.'

Joe and Terry started out as a team. Then came the disagreement. Joe decided to head to the barn, but Terry thought differently.

Rough began immediately.

Terry said he lost count how many times he pulled his face out of the dust and crawled back on that horse. But they finally came to a working arrangement. Horse let boy believe he was in charge, as long as boy was understanding and agreeable to what horse wanted.

Scripture tells us to not brag about tomorrow, because we don't know what tomorrow may bring. The last few years have been a living testimony to that. "Better get a deep seat and a tight hold, 'cause things can likely get a little rough." In other words, go ahead and enjoy right now, but prepare yourself for tomorrow's worst, the best that you can. Though all may be well today, changes come in a heartbeat. It's called LIFE.

CODDLING IS A KILLER

Early in our marriage, we were both employed at a large feed, seed and fertilizer company. Its walk-in store was extremely busy from local traffic in the spring, due to the seed and garden plants it carried. Andy was a salesman on the floor, while Renie worked in the offices.

One morning in early spring, Andy sold a dear lady several beautiful, healthy-looking tomato plants. Satisfied with her purchase, she left determined to grow a bumper crop of vine-ripened tomatoes.But some weeks later he looked up to see her stomping back into the store, the dark look on her face giving Andy immediate clues that he was going to be facing a thunderstorm. Complete with threatening lightning bolts and terrifying wind.

Seems the lady's bumper-tomato dreams had turned into a tomato-less nightmare, and she not only demanded an explanation and an apology, but she also wanted a full refund of her money.

Andy listened patiently and then actually called the company owner for his input. Surprisingly, the owner immediately left his office and walked onto the floor of the store (he probably wanted to see the source of all the loud hubbub.) When she finished her angry tale of woe, he then began to question the treatment and care of her beloved plants. Soil, watering amounts, and sunshine...basic issues of gardening.

Evidently having enough of his questions, she finally yelled, "I have done everything EXACTLY like I was told to do when I bought those plants! Not only that, but I have babied and cared for those plants, and protected them from every possible thing that might harm them. And they still won't put on even one lousy bloom."

The owner then proceeded to shock the poor woman when he calmly stated, "Well, ma'am, what I suggest you do is go home, take your water hose and whip the daylights out of those pampered plants." Horrified, the lady indignantly exclaimed, "What? You want me to beat up my babies? Well, I never!"

Amused at her response, he replied, "Yes ma'am, that is precisely the problem... you didn't. Your over-protective care has created a perfect environment for those plants. But every plant must have a certain amount of stress - it causes them to produce fruit. You've told me they are large, lush and beautiful, but have produced nothing. So, go stress 'em."

Glaring angrily, with some huffing and puffing thrown in, she finally stomped out - never to be seen again.

Learn this. We humans, just like in the plant world, also need a certain amount of struggle in our life. Why? Because if not for stress and difficulties, we would stay just like that lady's pampered tomato plants. Green and lush, but honestly, not producing much. So, God allows problems in our life to strengthen and mature us, to the point of being able to act like responsible adults who can contribute to society.

Hmmmm, come to think of it, those coddled plants remind me of so much of our country today.

FREE BELLY LAUGHS

I can be sitting at my desk, deeply engrossed in thinking of a serious crisis the world is facing. My mind spiraling downward in never ending circles, like water going down a drain. And as I contemplate the seemingly unsolvable issue that has my attention, if I am not careful, the problem can consume my morning. Like beef jerky - the more I chew on it, the tougher it gets.

But suddenly, out of the blue, I hear the happy-go-lucky giggle of a toddler at play. And the murky gray space around me seconds before suddenly lightens just a little.

A child's laughter, the simple enjoyment of what they are doing right then holds no guile, no worry, no pretense, no shame or embarrassment. It is the expression of what they are feeling. Fun. Happiness in the moment. Innocent appreciation of their life right now.

One of the greatest sounds in the world is laughter. It can surpass wind rustling through the trees, thunder rolling in the distance, and rain pattering on the roof while I am falling asleep – and these are personal favorites of this writer. But nothing holds a candle to hearing the laughter of happy children.

The scripture teaches that "Laughter doeth good like a medicine." Modern scientists can list many health benefits in laughter. Known to be a great stress-reducer, causing dormant feel-good endorphins to kick in and change our mood. It is also known as a pain reliever and immune system booster, so this free medicine is nothing to ignore.

This hurting world could use a good old-fashioned belly laugh about now. And I'm not talking about bullying or cruelly having fun at the expense of someone else. Just the emotional release found in finding humor in ourselves and the situations around us.

When our two sons were small, the oldest could tickle the funny bone of the toddler with such simple things. We would hear his infectious baby laughter break out in their room they shared. When one of us would step to the door, we would find the youngest sitting spraddle-legged on the floor, giggling at the smallest inane things his brother would be doing. Placing a tiny crumb of his cookie on his baby brother's lip could cause uncontrolled hilarity to erupt from both of them. Silly, of course. Of no consequence, absolutely. Notable in this world, not a chance. But bonding? Without a doubt. Healthy? No doctor would disagree.

Oh yes, I realize we are no longer innocent fun-seeking children anymore. You and I have jobs with responsibilities that carry serious weight. And I am very much aware that we live in a broken hurting world, with so little to find funny anymore. But that is precisely my point. You need to laugh. You need to seek out the silly, the laughable, the worry-breaking, the tension-lifter… however you can find it without causing harm.

Oh, one more great benefit of laughter? It is so contagious. Listen to the wholesome lighthearted chuckles of a group of adults and see if it doesn't lift the mood of everyone around them. But speaking of contagion. Watch what happens when a group of serious-minded and worried adults get together for a discussion. Feel the tension escalate. Watch the worry growing in their eyes. Visualize the rising blood pressure. Imagine the accumulating effects on stress levels and strained immune systems. Not a pretty picture.

So, what has made you laugh recently? Talking about a full throttle throw-your-head-back-and-enjoy-the-moment laugh at something you find just plain funny. Don't remember? Never have? Think that idea is rather useless and shallow? Hmmm.... maybe you could learn something from an innocent child. Someone who already knows how to enjoy life in the moment with absolutely no expense attached.

By the way, have you heard the old joke "Knock, knock...?"

I CAN'T FIND IT

"I can't find it," he cried... again... from the kitchen.

"It's there, just where I told you it was the last time you needed it," his wife resignedly said...again...from the living room.

He had gone to the kitchen to find a particular item. She had told him the cabinet and exact shelf, and yet he still couldn't locate it...again.

This scene has been played and replayed a great many times throughout their marriage. He is looking, she is giving directions, until finally they both give up. Then she stomps directly to the cabinet and retrieves the item that has, according to the husband, just magically appeared on that shelf. Silently his wife hands it over, but there seems to always be a sarcastic smirk lingering around the edges of her wordless mouth.

Men, it has to be a 'guy blindness' thing - or else women own super powers that they have never admitted to having.

This I-can't-find-it problem reminds me of so many people who are looking for help and direction. They search and search, and yet cannot locate what it is they are looking for in life. Others around them can attempt to give them direction, and sometimes there are a few among those seekers who do listen. They hear, follow the advice, and begin to walk a path that is better suited for them.

But all too often the searcher doesn't seem to even have a desire or a clue how to listen and then heed instruction. Honestly, there seems to be a mental block that keeps them from hearing what they have been told.

In many cases, those same people don't seem to realize and believe that there is an even more reliable source than family or friends for getting instructions. God's Holy Word. Jeremiah 33:3 says, "Call unto Me, and I will answer thee and show you things you do not know." Jesus states in Matthew 7:7, "Ask, and it shall be given you; seek and ye shall find; knock and it shall be opened to you." Folks, how much plainer can He have made it?

But there is a caveat, a qualification, to these directions and promises. They are made for God's children. Someone outside the family? Does not apply. Yes, I hear your protests, that He loves everyone and we are all His. It is true, everyone is His creation and He loves them.

But the only people He calls His children are those who have accepted Jesus as Savior and Lord. Please do not take offense at this. Remember, He also said, "Whoever calls on the name of the Lord shall be saved." (Romans 10:13) You may not know Him now, but I promise you, anyone can become part of that family that He guides so carefully.

GOOFBALLS, BULLIES, AND THE REST OF US

Ever wonder why goofballs walk this earth? You know them, not a serious thought in their head for more than fifty-eight seconds at a time. They believe that life is a playground, and they need to enjoy each ride that exists. And taking on a serious role, where they have to act the part of the heavy? "Not happening, dude! That's not the way I roll!" But we absolutely love having them in our lives, anyway. They have the ability to bring light and laughter wherever they go.

Why are they here? When there is so much at stake? When children are being abused, nations are being plundered, and countless people are losing everything they have worked for years to acquire. What is the goofball's contribution that will help this hurting world?

Well, first of all, ain't none of our business why God decided to make that particular version of His creation. We are to believe He knows what He is doing, and He's making sense of it all. Whether or not we understand it or agree with Him.

But, if I had to hazard a guess, and believe me it is only a guess, it would be this:

What if everyone on earth were exactly like you or me in personality? Oh my. Just the thought makes me cringe. What if all of us were absent-minded, or serious to a fault, or perfectionists that drive everyone to want to drink, or legalists, or complainers, or any other personality quirk we see. We would quickly drive each other up the wall, or life would get very boring, and probably a lot of work would never get done.

We need each other. Warts and all. Every kind of person is essential to our life on earth. (Well, excepting homicidal sociopaths, I refuse to believe those kinds of traits are essential.)

There is the Sanguine – who rarely meets a stranger. Fun and outgoing, but can be impulsive and spontaneous at the worst possible time. The Melancholy – a creative type, but also prone to worry and angst. Then the Phlegmatic – agreeable, steady minded, considerate, warm, but with a tendency be a wee bit dramatic. And the Choleric – brave and ambitious, but also can be bossy, deceitful, irritable and a tad violent. The Supine – sweet and quiet, but can get their feelings hurt very easily.

And then there is all the rest of us, a mixture and blend of these major temperaments. Together we are a big ol' melting pot of people, with every trait, need, ability, strength, and fault that you can imagine. And every person is needed and has a function to play in our world. Just the way the Creator intended, I have to believe.

So, what do you do when the one next to you is being irritating?

Just sigh, hold your tongue and take a moment to try to imagine everyone approaching life just like you. Scary stuff. (That's enough to make you work a little harder to appreciate that coworker who's stomping on your last nerve.)

BOUNDARIES ARE MEANT TO BRING ABOUT NECESSARY PAIN

Our floors here in the Midwest get freezing cold in the wintertime. So cold that you really can't just ignore them. There is no, "I'll just mosey into the kitchen in my bare feet and get me a cup of coffee and make myself a sandwich. It's only minus 15 degrees on my tile floor." Nope, there is something about bare feet suddenly hitting a biting-cold surface. You get a lightning strike to your senses, the old preservation instinct kicks in, and most of us immediately find a way to avoid that cold. Like jumping from the couch to chair, and then to another chair to get back where it's safer.

All of us have ways of dealing with our cold surfaces. We may carpet it or heat it, or wear shoes 24/7. But for some strange reason, there are moments when we decide to risk it. We act like an idiot and streak to the kitchen au naturel on tiptoe, shrieking our pain at the top of our voice. But mostly, we just stick to our tried-and-true methods that guarantee the warmest and safest way to go.

But sometimes stupid does just kick in....

Reminds a person of living. Sometimes your life just flows along easily, and you walk along enjoying warmth and a certain amount of comfortability. Then you suddenly find yourself walking a subzero portion of life. And hopefully you scramble to find a way back to what has been working better for you.

It is called recognizing boundaries. We find them in our floors and in life. And when we cross those barriers, we know it soon enough. Brutal cold wakes you up like nothing else.

Folks, when it pertains to cold floors, we basically are in charge. We determine whether we protect our toes, or push those boundaries and tiptoe on freezing bare feet. And that is a metaphor for the rest of our physical life. Drive too fast and end up getting a ticket. Spend money foolishly and have to dig ourselves out of debt for the next five years. Choose to have an unwise relationship and have it winding up hurting us. Eat too much all the time….

All of the above are examples of choosing not to recognize boundaries.

But our spiritual life? We determine how close we live to our God, whether we decide to live in obedience or in rebellion, and our Heavenly Father acts as our freezing cold floor.

He has boundaries in place for us. Painful barriers to alert us that we are straying. But why does He allow us to stray at all? To teach and train us. The other function of those unexpectedly painful encounters with boundaries. Primarily, we learn that we won't die from pain, even though it feels that way. But then gradually, we learn and then actually begin to do things differently.

Example: Place a person barefoot on a painfully cold surface for the very first time and you will probably hear gasping and loud shrieking. That person will make a quick retreat their only priority. But someone who has been there many times before? That person will eventually begin to think along the lines of, "Why do I keep doing this? This is stupid! I'm buying me some fuzzy slippers, 'cause I hate this!"

Same thing happens in life. And that is when change for the better happens. Called M-a-t-u-r-in-g.

Nobody we know likes walking barefoot on freezing floors in the wintertime. And most of the time we will finally do something about it. So, a painful boundary does bring about change… eventually.

II

PRIDE, PREJUDICE AND OTHER PROBLEMS WITH US

RUN THAT FOOL MULE!

Growing up on a small farm, Andy and his dad worked some long hours together. But sometimes they just relaxed, "Sittin' spittin' and whittlin', as his dad called it. Those times were more than just the obvious conveyed by that name. His dad used them to teach his son tidbits of wisdom. To illustrate his point, dad would often tell a story. Like the time he wanted Andy to remember, "There will always be someone in your life to tell you what you can't do... even while you are doing it." He then told his son this less-than-extremely-believable tale.

"An old Alabama farmer entered the local coffee shop of the small town. Spotting a group of his buddies at a table, he joined them for a lazy session of hot coffee, tepid gossip, and outright stone-cold lies. Pretty soon, over the brim of his cup, one old-timer eyed him curiously and then asked, "Where ya been lately, Clem? Ain't seen ya 'round heah in several days."

Clem never looked up from staring at his own coffee in front of him on the table. Taking his time answering, he finally drawled, "Waal, I took ol' Jake, my mule, up to Looweeville."

"Why'd ya take 'em all the way up there? Is he sick or sumpin?"

"Naw, Jake ain't sick or nuthin'. I just took him to run in that theh Kaintucky Derby."

Everyone at the table stared in astonishment and unbelief, until finally a rush of adrenalin loosened their tongues.

"Ya did what? Ya can't do that!"

"Are ya crazy, ya can't run that dumb ol' mule in th' Derby!"

"Clem, ya' old fool! Jake's jus' a mule, he shore don't belong in no thoroughbred horse race!"

On and on it went, the jibes and the laughter at Clem's expense. Until finally Clem raised his head and with a gleam in his eye he replied, "Waal, I'm shore glad you fellas didn't say all this to Jake, cause he might'a been too scairt to try, and never won that whole &#*@ race!"

Oh yeah, admittedly the story was a bit embellished. But still, Andy's dad was right. There will always be someone around to discourage you from trying to accomplish something unique. And if you make the fatal mistake of listening to these "just being realistic" voices in your life, you can end up too discouraged to even try.

Remember; your success or failure can often depend upon whose voice inside your head that you choose to heed.

If you have a dream, then dream. Expand your ideas. Study all angles. Do a lot of research on the subject. If it seems to still hold all the possibilities that you originally thought it would, then approach a trusted acquaintance with your idea. Someone who will listen, and then encourage the positives, point out the problem areas to be fixed, and will refrain from ever trying to discourage you.

A mule might not ever get to win the Kentucky Derby. But look how much farther he would go in life, by being encouraged to simply try.

INSTRUCTION MANUAL? NAH, DON'T NEED IT

Men. The very first species of human-kind that the Creator made, and with absolutely no instruction manual to show Him how. The Bible says God made Man "in His image." I have to wonder - is that why men are so reluctant to read the instruction manual, or stop and ask someone for directions? Was God so literal about man being made in His image, that a man has a built-in "Nope, don't need it" in their DNA?

Ever noticed the first thing the average man does when he has purchased and unboxed an item that needs assembling? Yep, you got it. He will immediately toss the packing Styrofoam into the trash, along with the printed INSTRUCTIONS FOR ASSEMBLING. Then he will spend the next few hours muttering and grumbling as he repeatedly tries and retries to make the pieces, various bolts and all the screws fit. And then when -and if- he finally gets it all put together in a semblance of the original intent of the item, he probably will have a screw left over. At which point he triumphantly holds it up and yells to his wife, "They did it again! They invariably send at least one too many! I think they must do that to mess with your head."

"Written instructions from the manufacturer are there to help you correctly assemble and use the item." That sentence is a simple explanation of why following the item's manual is the easiest, fastest, and smartest way to succeed. Easy enough to understand the concept. Then why do most men make certain that the first thing to hit the bottom of the trashcan is said manual?

Refer to my earlier sarcastic comment - their DNA?

Bet you Bible-reading women already know where this is going. But I'll continue on for the benefit of all.

To have a good and loving marriage. To successfully rear children and be a great dad. To be the best that you can be at your chosen field of work. To be a godly man, husband and father. YOU GOTTA READ THE INSTRUCTION MANUAL THAT TELLS A MAN HOW TO DO IT. Men, you don't have to just wing it – striking out on your own, doing the best that you can with no instructions. That would be a pretty unfair expectation, and God didn't do that.

In His infinite wisdom your Creator knew you would need help. You have a difficult job ahead of you – being the leader of your home, a godly example and guide for your kids to follow. That's why He gave you an instruction manual. Your Bible.

Like my mom used to yell, "Do ya think I'm just talkin' to hear my voice in the wind? I'm tryin' to help you!"

Same with your Creator. He wants to help you with all the hard stuff in life.

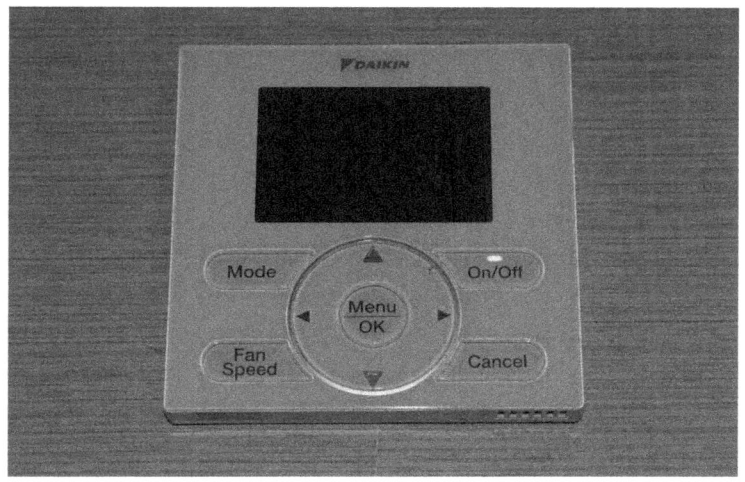

IS SHE THE ONLY LIVING PERSON IN THE ROOM?

Sometimes you just have to shake your head and laugh. 'Cause certain people in a church can be downright funny.

More than once, I have quietly stood in an out-of-the-way corner and watched as a dear church member walked into the auditorium. This self-centered individual heads directly to the thermostat on the wall closest to her favorite pew, and arrogantly adjusts it to her individual preference. Apparently believing that everyone else has her taste in room temperature. Or just blatantly disregarding the comfort level of anyone else whose internal thermostat may run at least fourteen degrees lower than hers.

Unmistakable message? "Don't make a hill of beans difference to me what anyone else in here wants…I'm BURNIN' UP!" Not funny yet.

The funny part? This person seemingly does not realize that more often than not, in that smallish church auditorium the thermostat she adjusts so zealously does not affect her area of the room. It usually blows over to the other side of the auditorium, while the thermostat on the opposite side of the room adjusts the temperature in her area. But psychologically she feels better, because the lowered thermostat tells her it is going to quickly get cooler. So, she settles in to a pew and gets comfortable.

But now the people on the other side are not appreciating the sudden drop in temperature. Invariably, one of them will look around and notice that people nearby are now sitting on their hands and looking a little anxious. So, this good neighbor makes his way to the nearest thermostat to adjust the temperature upward. And so it goes. The weekly weather war of the saints begins. One of these days, there's gonna be a sudden downburst of rain right down the middle aisle, from all that cold air meeting hot air.

Another unfunny side of all this?

We all look to make ourselves comfortable in life, many times with very little thought or consideration for how our actions may affect others. Way too often we insist that our personal preferences be honored. And when it comes differing opinions, we will argue as if "This is straight from the mouth of God." But Jesus said to love thy neighbor as you love yourself. Somehow the translation of that verse into our real behavior seems to get lost.

The Apostle Paul wrote, "I can eat the meat; but if it offend my brother to eat meat, I will not eat it...ever." What was he saying? Just because you can have your way, just because there is nothing wrong with your way, does not mean that you should insist on your way, if it will bring a problem to another person.

So, before you demand that your church and the world around you respect your rights and opinions on any given subject, you might pause and realize that some of your choices are probably impacting someone else. And not in a good way.

Just a thought.

BULLYBIRDS

On a lovely spring morning last year, we were on our back deck enjoying a cup of coffee, and looking over the flower garden. The butterflies were flitting around it and the birds were singing in the trees nearby. Everything seemed so lovely and peaceful...then there he was. A cute little hummingbird made a beeline directly to the fountain in the middle of the garden. He perched himself on the top tier and began to drink and bathe in the spray. Not bothering a soul around him, he was just having a high ol' time.

Suddenly out of nowhere, a slightly bigger hummingbird dove at the first one and drove away our contented little feathered friend. We watched as the second bird flew away after he had successfully driven off the small one. But in a minute, after the bully bird had left the fountain, the first little hummingbird returned to bathe and drink. Only to be driven away again by the same aggressive bigger bird.

We sat and watched this scenario play out repeatedly for a while, and repeated again the next morning. But by day three, something unique took place. As before, when the first little bird settled in the water, the bullybird drove directly at him. But this time something else happened. Three more hummingbirds appeared and intercepted Mr. Bully and allowed the little one to finish his bath! The bully was actually stopped by these other hummingbirds on behalf of the small one.

In most walks of life there is a bullybird type person in the group. They can be found in any kind of group; civic, family, or church. Many times, they are the first to speak up and they do it loudly, in a subtle attempt to control and impose their will on all the others. This is usually a technique used to quell any opposing thoughts and opinions from being voiced. They realize most people tend to be non-combative, and usually are not willing to cause dissension and problems, especially when faced with a bully.

But just like the hummingbirds, bullied people can learn to stand together and take care of each other. They can care enough for the others around them to put an end to bullybirds controlling the group or organization. Like those hummingbirds in the above story, many times they only need to stand together and the bully will often retreat to a safer perch. Or that bully may learn to see things a little differently and decide to join everyone else and play nice. In that case, everyone wins.

I DON'T NEED HELP, I GOT THIS!

Our family traveled a lot years ago, singing on Sunday morning in churches in another states. Back in those days, when you attended church, you were expected to dress more formally than is accepted today. Therefore, this entailed having to pack suits, ties, and dresses, along with 'non-church clothes.'

As mom, Renie had always overseen our sons' selections and the actual packing, making certain that they had what they would need. But when our oldest son was a teenager, the inevitable time came when he began to feel the need to be in total control of his destiny. To spread his fledgling wings and began to learn to fly on his own. So, when the time came to pack, he informed her, "Mom, I got this."

Typical hovering mother bird of an inexperienced baby bird wanting to leave the nest, Renie went back upstairs to remind him of a few things he would need on the trip. With indignantly ruffled feathers on weakly flapping wings, he responded, "MOM! I told you, I got this! I know what I'm doing." Hurt feelings and all, momma bird quietly returned to her own packing. Not reassured that he would actually have everything he would need, but resolved to let her baby bird learn to fly.

All went well on the trip with the family having fun together for a few days. Until Sunday morning. About ten minutes before we were to open the service with a happy praise song, we looked around the auditorium…no Brian. Andy went to search the Men's rooms, while Renie scoured the public areas…no Brian.

So, we extended the search to outside, where we quickly found him. Sitting very quietly in the front passenger seat of our van, wearing the proper suit and tie. His rather upset Dad wanted to know what he thought he was doing, when Brian knew he needed to be in the auditorium ready to sing in just a few minutes. Brian never looked up. He simply extended one foot out the van door – a foot wearing his favorite bright red, high-top Chuck Converse Allstars. Of course, his mom asked the obvious, "Where are your dress shoes?" His shame-faced answer was, "Back in my closet, I guess."

Having no choice, little bird sang that morning with his red high-tops peeking out below his suit and tie. No big deal, and actually got quite a chuckle from the crowd that morning. But it served as a reminder of how an attitude of rebellion and pride can cause consequences.

President Woodrow Wilson, known for his high intelligence, once said of his presidency, "I'm smart enough to use all the intelligence of everyone I can get around me." That man knew enough to realize he didn't know everything, and to take advantage of what was offered to him by others.

"I got this," sure sounds self-confident, but can lead you to ignore the advice of others who only have your best interests at heart.

I SHORE 'NUFF HATE IT WHEN THE WIFE GETS SICK

The following is a man's recipe for eventually learning to live all alone…

"Shoot, I really hate it when the wife's feelin' bad. It jest gets her down and seems to mess up her days. I've watched it thru the fifty years of our marriage, so I know what I'm a'sayin' to be true.

Recently, I got up one early frosty mornin' when she was sick, and bless her heart, she had yet to stoke the fire. And she also had let the supply in the wood box run out. I shore feel bad for her when she lets that happen. 'Cause I know she plumb dislikes havin' to go out on th' back porch, - that's where she stacks it - to get another armload of wood. That cold air jest seems to make her a mite cranky. And speaking of mornin' chores, guess she also forgot to let our little dog out at 5:30, 'cause I saw a real mess on the carpet that she never likes cleanin' up.

Like I said, I shore hate it for her when she don't feel real good.

I told our kids to be extra kind 'n patient with her that mornin.' Told 'em they needed to remember that their momma don't move so quickly with a temperature of 103. I 'splainified to those little 'uns that we got to give her a little extr' grace and understandin.' We'll just sit quietly at the breakfast table if she's runnin' a little behind with our eggs and bacun. And if the biskuts are a little on the crunchy side, jest don't complain. She shore don't need the whole bunch of us a'tellin' her how bad they turned out, so jest let me do the talkin'.

She must've also been feelin' a mite poorly the evenin' before, 'cuz she plumb forgot to wash Junior's basketball uniform. So I made sure to warn the kids they wuz gonna be late for school - always seems to take so long for her to wash and dry that thing. Shore glad I've been workin' on larnin' patience.

But honestly, one of th' other reasons I hate it when my Sugar Bear comes up sick is– I have to milk old Bessie myself those days. And that cow never cooperates with me – guess she don't like strangers with cold hands. Makes me feel downright un'ppreciated.

Yep, th' wife is in my prayers today. I shore 'nuff hope she starts feelin' better soon, cause it's gettin' close to tillin' and plantin' time, and that woman jest has a special way with our ol' tractor. Guess 'cause she's worked on it for so many years when it breaks down.

I shore do hate it when that woman of mine gets sick, I truly do.

Go ahead and laugh at this guy, but treat your own spouse with the kindness and respect that love demands!

DISASTROUS DOG-DIPPING DAYS

If you have ever wanted to ask a couple how they have successfully stayed married for many decades, then this one is for you.

This is a story from Doug and Joan, who have been weathering the storms of life together for over fifty years. Granted, many of those storms came from the hand of Someone who knew they needed the pressure to make them grow together as a couple, but others were definitely man-made. This couple has walked thru them all together…just maybe not hand-in-hand all the time!

Recently Joan gave us another true story of what life dumped on their doorstep:

"Many years ago, when Doug started traveling a lot doing work all over Texas, he was gone a good deal of the time. Which left me and our two young daughters at home alone. In view of this, he decided to get a dog to protect us while he was gone.

We bought a black chow and named him Rascal. Besides being a good watch dog and a great companion, he was one of the most beautiful dogs I had ever seen. But that long, thick, black hair was so hard to keep groomed. We lived close to a pasture and before long he was covered in ticks. With all that hair, bathing him was simply not keeping the ticks off.

Frustrated, one day I called the vet and asked him for help. But he wanted about $50 to dip him in a solution bath – which was quite a bit of money for a young family back in those years. So, my entrepreneurial husband decided he would save that money and fix the problem himself.

Doug got the horse watering trough, filled it with water (and for those of you who have a 'Doug,' you know he has never measured anything in his life) and poured the entire bottle of tick removal solution into it. Eighty pounds of squirming Rascal was dumped in and held down with one arm, while Doug's other hand doused him thoroughly with the solution water. Afterwards we rinsed him off, then watched as a rather fragrant-smelling dog ran around the yard until he was dry.

In a few days we noticed his beautiful hair was falling out. Our gorgeous guard dog quickly became the ugliest half bald thing you have ever seen. Eventually, his hair did start growing back… but it was a rusty red color. Our gorgeous black chow was now covered in an ugly black and red combination. (Good wife that I am, I don't think I ever said, "I told you so" to Doug. But needless to say, I never let him dip or bathe another animal…)"

Then she told me the rest of the story.

"It was all so sad, but the following months were absolutely heartbreaking. When Rascal was beautiful, everyone loved being in his presence. But when he became ugly, those same neighbors suddenly refused to go near him."

Same dog and same personality, but when he became ugly, he brought a totally different reaction from folks. A depressing commentary on people's attraction to beauty over substance?

III

MARRIAGE AND THUNDERSTORMS: BOTH FROM HEAVEN

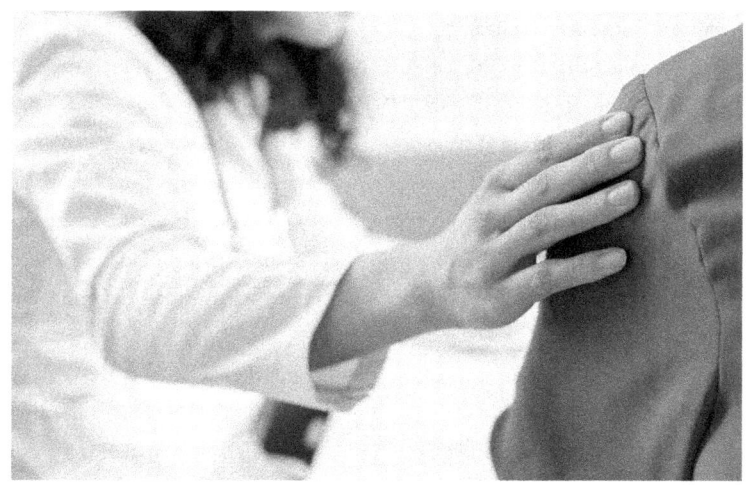

DON'T DO THAT IF IT HURTS

Several years ago, a pastoral counselor developed a "hitch-in-his-get-along."

Back when he was playing racquetball on a regular basis and competing in heated games, he had run his shoulder full speed into the concrete sidewall. Weeks later, the pain from that close encounter still hadn't left and finally forced him to visit his doctor.

The doctor's examination involved the necessary moving and rotating of the man's arm to find out exactly what had happened internally. As Doc would lift the arm, the man would grimace with the pain.

To which the doctor would ask, "That hurts when I lift it?"

"You better believe it."

"Then be sure you don't do that."

The same exchange would happen again and again as the good doctor examined, probed, lifted, and pushed. Finally, the medical doctor told the counselor that his shoulder had only been severely sprained. He needed to refrain from causing any more damage by not doing anything that would cause him pain. In fact, it would benefit from not being used for a while. Prescription:

Just let it rest so it could heal.

The man left that day with a clear understanding – if he did something that caused his shoulder to hurt, DON'T DO THAT.

Years passed, and that story became part of his counseling arsenal. As he watched pain-filled married couples enter his office seeking counseling, he found himself referring back to those days of shoulder trauma. Back to his doctor telling him, "If what you are doing causes pain in that shoulder, you need to stop doing it. It can, and probably will, create more serious or permanent damage than you've already done."

He would tell the story to hurting couples and then add, "If whatever you are doing is hurting your marriage, stop doing that! You need to realize that long-term damage results, if you callously persist in a behavior that is hurtful. Every once in a while, you need to stop and ask your spouse, 'Are you happy overall with what I am doing in this marriage?' Openly and carefully, listen to the response. Then do your best to make those changes needed."

Other times, frustrated and concerned parents would bring in young Johnny or Susie, asking for help with their troubling behavior. They were aware that childhood has consequences in approaching adulthood, and they sincerely wanted help. He would tell them that there had to have been a trauma somewhere. And it needed to be uncovered and stopped in its tracks, so healing can begin.

Folks, this needs to be heard - loud and clear; if something is happening that is causing pain, it needs to be stopped before it can create more serious or permanent damage.

Like his medical doctor said, STOP IT."

Find the problem, stop what is irritating it, and allow healing to begin.

ARE MEN REALLY JUST THAT BLIND?

The husband was preparing his own lunch that day. His wife wasn't feeling well, so he was on his own. He decided he would open up a can of soup, add a few crackers, and he'd be just fine.

The rest of the story, according to him…

"Put soup in bowl, heat in microwave. Add crackers and eat, Easy, peasy, right? But a few hours later my sweet fever-ridden wife wandered into the kitchen. Then it began. She was definitely not impressed with my kitchen skills. Oh, what I had fixed for myself was no problem, she was happy that I am capable of fending for myself. But her problem was the way I had left the kitchen after I had gone back to my office with my stomach full.

Now, let me be clear, folks. I have good eyesight, it has been checked recently and I am clear to read, write and drive, just like any other adult male. So, strongly believing in my abilities, I defiantly stood up for myself and my cleaning skills. I felt like telling her that she has the eyes of an eagle on the hunt for baby sugar ants on a tree-covered mountain slope. But I resisted that stupid impulse, and simply told her that I certainly had cleaned up after myself. Then her eyes began to squint slightly with that oh-too-familiar-look of "Ohhhhh, really?"

Then she started pointing. Uh-oh.

Sticky drips of soup left all over the counter top. Splattered soup inside the microwave, (Yeah, I forgot to cover the bowl.) Cracker crumbs left to populate the island where I ate. My empty bowl and glass left in the sink for someone else to wash. And somehow someone - who shall remain nameless to protect the guilty - had dropped hot sauce on the floor to evaporate or clean itself.

May I simply say that my ill and fatigued wife was not a happy camper?

The following one-sided conversation included comments along the lines of, "are men just blind slobs...my heritage... my degree of intelligence," and some other flattering observations.

I didn't knowingly leave a dirty kitchen. Nor did I deliberately leave it for her to clean. But I did make a mess and then walked out. And left it for someone else to clean up. I had been thoughtless and careless, absorbed in my thoughts concerning a project, and simply didn't take the time to check behind myself before leaving the room.

This may sound a lot like what happens in many other homes. Someone in the household creates a problem or a mess. Not intentionally, but it happens. And because that person doesn't recognize it as a problem, someone else has to deal with the aftermath. Even if the guilty party cleans up their own mess after it's brought to their attention, it can leave a bad taste in the mouth of the other people around them. There usually are no good outcomes from that scenario. Definitely does not do positive things for relationships.

So, learn to look behind you. Clean up your own mess. Take responsibility for you. And when you do make a mistake, apologize to each other.

THE COUNSELOR GRABBED HER AND KISSED HER

A troubled couple went to see a marriage counselor. After many sessions with unsuccessful attempts to get the couple to view their problems in the same way, the counselor was feeling frustrated with their stonewalling.

The day came when the unhappy wife simply blurted out, "I just need to feel swept off my feet with love and passion and romance." In one swift move the counselor stood and pulled her to her feet. Bending her backward in his arms, he proceeded to kiss her thoroughly with great passion. He then sat the now swooning wife back into the chair beside her husband.

Hoping that he might have finally gotten through to the man, the counselor turned to face the husband and said with a smile, "And that, sir, is what your wife needs about three times a week." To which the husband hesitantly drawled, "O-k-a-yyy…guess I can bring her by Mondays, Wednesdays and Fridays."

Several years ago, Gary Chapman wrote a great book, "The Five Love Languages." He pointed out that each of us have one particular way that makes us feel loved, more than any other. Some people feel a need for (1) words of affirmation, others thrive on (2) physical touch. There are many who feel loved when they receive (3) gifts, and others need (4) acts of service done for them. Then there those who respond best to (5) time together.

If you have a relationship with someone, then you want that person to feel loved by you. And in return, you also want and expect that someone to do the same. But for this to happen, each of you need to know what knocks your socks off. While also realizing that your own love language probably doesn't do a thing for your partner's socks.

Here's some examples of the problem. You may be a female who knows that receiving an expensive gift simply sweeps you off your feet. So unthinkingly, you assume the same works for your loved one. Au contraire, my assuming friend! If he's someone who feels loved when there is a hot meal on the table and clean socks and underwear in his dresser drawer, then you will have totally missed the mark when you spend seventy-five hours a week working to buy him a Rolex watch.

And if you are one of those word-loving husbands who depend on calling your touchy-feely wife six times a day to say "I love you," while you spend your down-time fishing or hunting with the guys, you probably just should go ahead and call a divorce lawyer instead of her.

Want a thriving relationship? Learn! Ask what your loved one needs. And take the time to discover what makes you feel loved. Then learn to talk openly about what you both want from the relationship – unless you both have ESP, which I seriously doubt.

If you assume to know what your spouse needs, you can easily assume wrong, and eventually see your loved one searching for the nearest exit. And leave you scratching your head and wondering what in the world went wrong.

MARRIAGE CAN BE LIKE COFFEE AND CREAMER

Andy sits down every morning to enjoy his first cup of the day... (there will be more to follow, trust me.) Because he prefers coffee with creamer, he pours in a little and tastes it to make certain it is nicely proportioned to his specifications. That creamer can be the cheap powdered stuff or a gourmet blend, it doesn't really matter too much to him. Just so his coffee cup holds a perfect blend of both flavors. He insists that neither one be overpowering, that both be very present and perfectly balanced.

How God intended a marriage relationship to be. Two unique people coming together. They may be totally different in demeanor, personality and temperament. But then the Holy Spirit begins working. And through the passing of time, God has a wonderfully interesting couple.

Is every couple just exactly like every other couple – carbon copies of a "perfect marriage?" No way. God is much more innovative and creative than that. Every couple has their own style and personality. Their marriage will be unique to only them. And it will work, if they will allow Him time to do what He can accomplish in their lives. But that means hanging in there during the rough times. Because that's when God is working on changing us. Smoothing our rough edges. Creating two people who can stand to be together for the long haul.

Jesus said, "The two will become one." But just exactly what does that phrase mean?

Do they lose their individuality? Is Ken no longer Ken, and Jennie no longer Jennie? There is now only Jenken? Of course not. Being part of a partnership that is seamlessly melded together doesn't destroy the partners as individuals. They should, and they definitely need, to hold on to their own likes and dislikes, their own hobbies and preferences in life. Each needs to see themselves as a unique person, who is complete and whole in themself.

And they have to view their partner the same way. They have to give each other room to be different. If they are going to have a healthy marriage, they need to respect the right of their spouse to see life from a totally opposite viewpoint. Which of course can lead to some, umm, very interesting conversations.

Otherwise, marriage can get very boring. Can you imagine you living with you twenty-four/seven? Never having your opinions challenged? Not once having the opportunity to be forced to see life from a differing point of view? Your marriage would probably take on a dreary shade of beige without any other spark of color. Part of the exciting nerve center of a marriage is differences between a couple. That is where the growth of two people happens. One person smoothing the rough edges of the other, but also sharpening where sharpening is needed.

The un-citing part is when they haven't ever learned to disagree respectfully, when they resort to screaming their opinions and never listening to their partner.

When Jesus said, "The two will become one," the "one" is meant to be in focus and purpose, to bless and honor both partners involved. Two individuals with separate identities that meld into something as wonderful as a colorful marriage relationship.

Yes, coffee is still exactly what it is.... coffee. And creamer…it's still creamer. But together, they marry to make a great hot drink.

SONG AND DANCE ON THE BATTLEFIELD

A young couple was deeply involved in the timeless dance of married couples since the first union centuries before, and I am not referring to sex. This was the dance of war. Each had taken a rigid angry stance on opposite sides of their ballroom. In fact, the battle for this championship had escalated to the point that, no matter what one said, the other was definitely going to disagree. No compromise, take no prisoners. Victory at any cost.

The other dancers in that ballroom, aka their kids, and their desires for a peacefully happy dance were now unimportant. The ballroom was an ugly scene of combat, and winning was the only thing that mattered.

Sound familiar? Probably. Anyone in a close relationship has very likely found themselves embroiled in a heated argument, and eventually decided their opinion is the only one that holds any worth.

This couple ended up in a marriage counselor's office, sitting on opposite ends of the couch. Backs ramrod straight, arms crossed, chins high, and eyes glaring. The counselor felt like he was watching an ugly ballet that he had seen too many times. And after he had listened and watched each sing and dance their part, he made two simple statements.

"The problem is not the problem. Wife, he isn't the problem, and husband, neither is she."

When that statement hit the icy air, their glares turned on him. Then he began to speak from experience and training.

"What you both are yelling about are only symptoms of the problem, not the real problem. For example, if your child woke one night with a very high fever, you would most likely cover her with cold compresses and give her baby Tylenol before calling the doctor. But that would not solve the real problem... the reason behind the high fever. Your doctor would have to take steps to find and treat the actual illness itself. So, let's just back up, start at the beginning, and do some work. Before this disease in your marriage escalates and causes enough symptoms to eventually cause the death of your marriage."

What is the difference between symptoms and real issues in marriage, you might wonder? Well, for example, a wife complains bitterly to her spouse that he has, once again, broken his promise to lock the doors at bedtime. It's not really an issue to him so he doesn't understand her fear, and he repeatedly forgets.

But if the careless husband does learn to lock the doors, will that address the underlying issue? Probably not. Because the anger over unlocked doors may be just a symptom. The real problem could very well be tied to a lack of security and love, in her deeply buried memories of a fear-filled childhood. And the husband's lack of understanding of what truly loving someone means.

Don't make the mistake of dealing with just symptoms only. It won't solve the true problem, no matter how hard you try. Kind of like the man who painted the well house a pristine white when the pump began delivering murky brown water into the house. His work didn't fix the problem of the bad water, but according to him, "It sure felt good to be trying to do something about it!"

BEWARE OF FORCING YOUR MATE TO COMPETE

The young man's bride of a whole six months waltzed dramatically into the den to show off her new outfit. But engrossed in the college football game of his alma mater, he never took his eyes off the screen. Slightly miffed, she moved in front of the tv to force him to notice her. Unfortunately, at the precise second she chose to make her move, his quarterback launched a thirty-yard pass that hopefully would tie the game. He let out a frustrated bellow, and certainly not really thinking of consequences, the young husband brusquely told her to move aside so he could at least see the replay.

Needless to say, the first argument of their young marriage began. Hours, and buckets of tears later, she finally admitted her fear, "It feels like you love football more than you love me!" Honest Abe should have thought just a few more seconds and made a fatal mistake when he blurted, "Oh, honey, that's just not true! And besides, I love you a lot more than basketball."

That night a little smarter Abe got well acquainted with the guest bedroom. Sometimes priorities can get a little off-center. The pleasure you get from that hobby can easily derail your common sense, and make you totally ignore what you know…that your loved one is more important than your hobby.

Be very wary if you find yourself pouring your time, or money, or even affection into what started out as a harmless pastime, but can end up as a hairy problem. And if it makes your loved one feel neglected and abandoned, you've got a hairy problem. Social media, sports, outdoor activities, and friends are all a good thing, if kept where they belong.… below your spouse on your list of 'I Want To Do This.' Otherwise, you are running the risk of damaging the very relationship that started out as Priority Uno.

Hobbies and side activities are a great thing, as long as they are just that – side stuff. Never let them become so important to you that your mate begins to feel jealous or abandoned. You are inviting consequences down the line that you are not going to enjoy. Here is why. Rare is the loved one who simply takes that kind of abuse quietly. Maybe not in a knockdown drag-out, they may be passive-aggressive in showing you their hurt feelings, but sooner or later those feelings will make their presence known.

Need some passive-aggressive examples? Mate starts looking for sly ways to hurt you. As in, bowling shirt got misplaced…hmmm, wonder how that happened? The spouse quits talking to you – or anything else. Or money is suddenly disappearing at a previously unknown rate into the pockets of local department stores. What used to be admiration and honor deteriorates into sniping and griping. Or some other irritating behavior that you will begin to notice in your relationship.

Realize, analyze, and be ready to apologize. Talk it out and compromise. You don't have to totally give up your hobby, you just need to put it in its proper place.

IT ALL STARTS WITH A STAND-OFF

Husband has had a horrible time at work that day. Feeling kicked around, unappreciated and definitely out of sorts, he pulls into the driveway, only to find that his three-year-old has left her tricycle blocking the garage door... again. He leverages his tired body out of the car and lumbers slowly into the house, ready to snap the head from the first person he sees.

Wife is loading the dishwasher when he walks in the kitchen, her tension headache competing for her attention amidst all the other hubbub. Their six-month-old sick baby is screaming in her arms, the pot of spaghetti is boiling over on the stove behind her, the seven-year-old twins are loudly fighting over the tv, and she accidentally left the handle of the dirty mop in his way to trip over.

Not exactly the calming scenario he was needing at that point. Tired, discouraged husband erupts in anger and frustration. Harried and exhausted wife, who has also put in a hard day at work and arrived home just an hour before him, responds in kind.

Can we say World War, with the twins disappearing up the stairs to play the role of Switzerland?

Who is at fault? A hurting husband and dad? A depressed, tired wife and mother? More importantly, which of them is going to make the first move towards apologizing and trying to see the situation from the other person's point of view?

And worse, what happens when neither adult decides to try to be the bigger person?

Well, Switzerland decides to eat spaghetti up in their bedroom. The sick six-month-old feels the tension, and that causes her to fret even louder. The three-year-old reacts to the negativity surrounding her and acts out the fear she feels building within. And husband and wife add another layer of resentment and anger to the wall that lately has been building between them.

If no one in this situation stops long enough to realize what is happening, and puts an abrupt halt to it all by putting their gun back in the holster, then the problem is probably only going to escalate in intensity. And when that kind of scenario happens often enough in a marriage, then those two pseudo-grownups will eventually begin to wonder if being in this union is worth it.

"I am so sick of this! And my kids? Shoot, they're acting out worse than ever before. Probably because all we ever do is fight around them. They'll be a lot better off if one of us just gets the heck out of here. After all, they're just kids, and everybody knows kids are flexible and adaptable. They would be just fine."

Yeah, right.

That's why we have so many depressed and angry kids who are being reared in single family homes. Why we have kids who are either having to adjust to being shuffled back and forth between Mom and Dad's houses, or have to live without the benefit of one of their parents in their life.

Parents, it is time to figure it out, whatever it takes. For your children's sake. Because regardless of what we have been told; kids suffer badly when mom and dad split up. Unless there is spousal or child abuse happening, it is far better for the kids when their parents stay together and make a tremendous effort to work out what is going wrong in their relationship. Sure it's hard! Any couple married for a lot of years will tell you that. But the emotional well-being of your kids is at stake here. If they could, I think they would tell you it is well worth the struggle you will have to go through.

A FIVE-HOUR FEAST YESTERDAY IS NO HELP TODAY

The couple sitting in the counselor's office had been married over forty years. They had weathered financial setbacks, the rearing of two children, moving from city to city due to job changes, and countless marital disagreements. But they had finally hit their last wall and in desperation, they had come to the point of consulting a marriage counselor. Now they sat in cold silence, as they waited for the therapist to join them.

Into this tense and silent setting walked the counselor, who seated himself and turned to the wife. "Mrs. Smith, in your opinion, what seems to be the root problem that has brought you and your husband to see me today?"

Tears of frustration filled her eyes as she bit her lip. Finally gaining control of her emotions she blurted,

"He never tells me he loves me! He just blabs on about everything else in our lives. And I am sick of being taken for granted! I need to be told that he loves me."

Staring in astonishment at his wife, the husband then yelled, "What are you talking about, woman? I most certainly have told you that I love you!"

Mrs. Smith shrieked back in frustration, "When? When did you tell me? You never tell me you love me!"

"On the day we got married, I said how much you mean to me and that I truly love you. And I told you then that if anything changed, I would let you know! Nothing has changed!"

If this is you, then maybe - just maybe - you might need to change your way of communicating.

A five-hour feast - forty years ago - of a person's favorite foods doesn't help that starving person today. And the words of affection you spoke to your spouse long ago doesn't do a blessed thing for right now. Most of us need to hear that we are loved just-a-leetle-more-often than that. Granted, you may be one of those strong silent types, not comfortable expressing your deep feelings. You prefer showing your love by doing, not talking. Understandable. Not disagreeing with that one bit. You are you.

But here is the problem: Your loved one needs you to give them those very words. Their ears and eyes feed their heart. And if the heart is starving, then a lonely hunger begins, and hunger feeds resentment.

This truth applies to more than spouses. Many a child goes through kidhood, never getting a lot of 'Atta-boy!' from his parents – and eventually growing into an adult with a lingering, deeply buried sense of frustration and low self-esteem. Parents, words of encouragement and love have more effect on the well-being of your child than anything else does in this life.

You have the power to give a loved one a great head-start on their day. Go ahead and praise little Johnny for only spilling his orange juice once at breakfast. Hug your prickly, sulky teenager as she flounces out the door. Stop rushing around, and make time to tell your spouse "I love you," before you head off to work.

Make their day brighter – and probably their life.

IV

CHOICES: YOU HAVE TO LIVE WITH THEM

WHEAT JEANS, A GIRL, AND JOHNSON GRASS

The little rural church always held its annual summer Vacation Bible School for kids. Each mid-morning, all those excited and rowdy kids were let outside for a few minutes for snacks and exercise. Balls were tossed around, and various games played until their exhausted teachers half-heartedly called them back inside.

That fateful morning, twelve-year-old Andy had proudly sported his new wheat-colored jeans to Bible School. Jeans that his mom had just purchased for returning to school in a few weeks. Knowing her son's ability to find every possible way to ruin his clothing, his mom had vehemently disagreed with Andy wearing them that day. But when he kept insisting that he would be careful, she finally relented. But with dire predictions of the stiff penalties he faced if his new jeans got damaged.

As they were summoned back to class after breaktime that warm sunny day, Quarterback Keith told his buddy Andy to "go for one more long pass." Andy immediately saw this as an opportunity to impress a certain young lady in his class with his considerable skills as a receiver. So with a grin, he started running while looking back over his shoulder, so he could track the progress of the ball.

In his imagination, he could hear an excited crowd roaring its approval and see the infatuated smile on little Becky's face. Seeing the football begin its final descent, he leaped as far as he could, stretched his arms out and was poised to make the catch on his fingertips. Sure enough, he cradled the ball safely in his hands as he hit the ground.

But.

At the edge of the church yard where the kitchen sink constantly drained, was a bog of foul-smelling, sticky mud. And always growing in that stinking mess was tall Johnson grass. It always effectively served as a constant warning to the kids, "DO NOT ENTER." Every child in the community knew to stop at the edge of that patch of high grass, or suffer the consequences.

But, evidently in preparation for the week of Bible School, a helpful someone had diligently mowed the Johnson grass. The boundary that Andy was accustomed to was gone.

There he landed, face down and fully stretched out in that nasty, stinking bog, where the tall grass should have been. Mud was in every orifice and covered his face. He instantly knew that his new wheat jeans were now his infamous Johnson Jeans. As he reluctantly raised his head up, he saw Becky disappear into the church. He also saw his mother stomping toward him, words describing his not-too-distant-and-unfortunate-future blazing from her lips.

Pretty careless and foolish of that young boy, ignoring the counsel and warnings of his mother. But even more foolish? To have just lain there in that stinking mess. To not bother to raise himself up, go home, strip off his ruined clothing, and find a nice hot shower.

Just like foolishly falling into a stinking mistake in life. It happens to us all at one time or another. But more foolish? To simply lie there in that filth.

Apologize to your God. Then get up, clean up and go again.

THE BED WAS ALREADY ON FIRE

A book title, "It Was On Fire When I Laid Down On It" caught my eye a few years ago. Curiosity being what it is, I looked up the story behind that title. True story. A small local fire department was called to put out a house fire. They also found and rescued a man trapped inside. Some days after his rescue, it was determined that the origin of the fire was the very mattress where he was found. Later, the local media asked the man about the cause of the blaze in that mattress.

Quote, "I don't know, it was on fire when I laid down on it."

What!!??

He knew the bed was smoldering, yet he laid his body down on that mattress and went to sleep anyway? This is truly hilarious and sad at the same time. Funny, because the visual just somehow tickles the funny bone. Sad, because it sounds way too much like some folks in this world. Danger ahead for them is as plain as the nose on their face. And yet, they plunge headlong onto 'the bed on fire already.'

Like the old boy who was struggling in his marriage. He knew that breaking up was not what he wanted. He didn't really want to face coming home to an empty apartment every night. But yet, for some reason he went ahead and got a tattoo of another woman's name on his stomach. Didn't exactly help his cause. Definitely 'bed on fire' when he did that.

Or when a woman decides to get into a relationship with a guy that has already lost two marriages due to domestic abuse – folks, she is jumping into "a bed already on fire."

When a person has already donated all his rent money to the casino and is borrowing more from his friend to double down. Oh, yeah, "the bed is on fire."

It is one thing when bad stuff happens that you can't see coming, and so you can't predict a bad outcome. That occurs to everyone at some point and it is inevitable. But, folks, when you can smell the smoke and see the flames, and yet you decide to go ahead and leap into that bed – that is insane! As the old saying goes; 'Learn to look before you leap.' But even better; 'Learn to look and sniff, and then don't leap.' Otherwise, you may wake up to find your life going up in flames. That's what happens when you know the bed is on fire, and yet you lay down on it anyway.

Choices: You Have to Live With Them

FENCES AND STUPID COWS

Ever had the opportunity to spend any time on the farm, or simply drive thru the country side? If so, you probably watched horses and cows grazing in pastures, and likely you have noticed something.

These animals do not like to stay where they were placed by their owner. And nobody really knows why.

Here's the frequently seen scenario. The farmer or rancher buys them, or raises them from birth. During the warmer months, he turns them out onto his fenced green pastures to graze to their heart's content. He makes certain they have access to water year around. When wintertime comes, he gives them expensive store-bought feed. When the harsh winter storms blow in, the owner provides shelter in the barn. That farmer will constantly patrol his animals, watching for any medical problems so he can catch and treat issues early.

Food, water, shelter and protection? What more could a four-legged creature want? Well, evidently, a lot more.

They seem to crave what is just beyond the fenced-in green pasture where they graze. That very fence that protects them from predators and fast-moving traffic. For some strange reason, the green grass they have no longer looks as good as what they see growing outside their pasture. It just seems to call out their name, convincing that idiotic cow that the grass just thirty six inches away is gonna taste a lot better than the grass at their feet. And somehow, that same stupid cow will find a way out of that pasture.

An internal hole-in-the-fence-seeking-radar must come standard on these animals. 'Cause if there is even just a six-inch opening in the fencing that surrounds the pasture, you can bet that cow can sniff it out. She will poke her head through that barbed wire, ignoring the pain from the cuts. Just to get a taste of what's outside the fence. Then she will nudge and squirm her bulky body through that hole, until she is totally free and standing outside of the fence's protection. The owner will likely find her next to a dangerous, heavily traveled highway, grazing peacefully. On grass that is probably a lot less quality than where she just left.

And even worse, these creatures of rebellion are training their offspring to do the same thing.

"See that thar fence, eva'body? That means only one thing. Ya' gotta find a way through it, over it, or 'round it. Cause that green stuff on the other side tastes a whole lot better than this grass at our feet. Prob'ly tastes a lot like chicken, or so I been told. So ya' just follow me, ladies."

Just like a lot of two-legged creatures. No matter how good life is, or how well the Creator has provided for us, some folks just can't stand to stay inside the fence. They see one blade of grass on the outside. "Oh, yeah, lookin' good!" Then a tiny hole of opportunity will present itself. And a stupid two-legged creature will ignore the painful warning cuts and will barge right on thru the fence. The very fence that is put in place by God to protect them from harm. Just to taste a mouthful of grass that is growing out there.

Probably directly over a septic tank.

CONSTANTLY RELIVING THE PAIN WON'T CHANGE THE PAST

Waking up that morning, she heard dripping outside the house. Opened the blinds of the bedroom window and saw a soggy lead-gray sky. Immediate reaction? "Oh, NO! Another horrible, gray, depressing, endlessly rainy day. I'm going to sink into depression. In fact, I'm already there."

Then the thought hit. 'You do have a choice, my dear. You can be gloomy and depressed all day about the cold and the rain, or you can remember that the grass and flowers need and love this.'

Perspective.

How we choose to look at a situation makes a huge difference. It determined why this lady turned on all the lights, put on happy music, and went to work feeling grateful for the heaven-sent automatic watering system. Much better than spiraling downward emotionally, into a dark quagmire of unhappy childhood memories of black, lonely, freezing, drizzly days.

If you are anything like the rest of us mere mortals, you have weaknesses, fears and emotional struggles. And if you don't wrestle with any of those attributes, then we would love to spend a few weeks tapping into your Super-Human-ness. Or more likely, have the opportunity to look you in the eye and call you a liar to your face.

Because the fact is, as human beings who live on planet Earth with all its pain and problems, every one of us have bad experiences. Those days leave their mark on our psyche in the form of painfully uncomfortable memories. And when something happens to trigger those memories and the feelings that result, then we have to make a choice. Wallow in the negative emotions, or realize we can deliberately choose to find a positive.

Difficult to do? Yes. Worthwhile to try? Absolutely.

After all, living through the actual situation that created the pain was bad enough, why make yourself relive that pain, anger and depression again and again? A much better choice is to somehow find gratefulness in that same memory.

Yes, I realize many of you reading this are hurting badly. And that grief and pain is not something to gloss over, but to walk through at your own pace. But your future peace and happiness will depend upon how you handle the ongoing memories of this depressing time.

Do yourself an enormous favor.

Accept that you have hurtful memories. Deliberately acknowledge those memories – don't refuse to admit they exist. Realize they have an extreme impact on your current emotions and thoughts. If possible, when the pain hits, work to find gratefulness in that memory. And dwell heavily on that gratefulness to change your mindset and your emotions. You can't change memories – only your perspective. And with perspective the memories do fade in intensity.

If you are not at the point in your life to be able to do this, then I beg you to seek out someone whom you can trust with your thoughts, and talk it out. A friend, a counselor, a pastor, or a person on the other end of a H-E-L-P Hotline. You are worth it.

IT'S JUST WHAT SNAKES DO

Do you remember the tale of the fellow who was walking down the road in front of his farmhouse one bitterly cold morning? He came across a small half-frozen poisonous snake lying in the grass nearby. The reptile pleaded in a weak voice, "Please sir, I am almost frozen to death. Could you please help me?"

The farmer felt a stir of pity, so he picked the creature up and placed him inside his warm jacket. Carefully cradling the snake, he then began the short walk back toward the house. Of course, in just a short time the snake started to warm up and began feeling back to his normal self. He then sank his fangs into the kind gentleman's flesh.

The farmer cried out in shock and pain, and reaching inside his jacket, he grabbed the reptile. "Why did you do that?! Now I will surely die!! I took you inside my own jacket when you were dying and gave you warmth, and you repaid my kindness like this!? Why??"

To which the snake calmly replied, "Yes, you will probably die. But you knew that I am a snake when you picked me up and put me in your coat. Yes, I bit you, 'cause that is what snakes do."

People often trifle with things and habits that are well known to hurt or destroy. If a guy ate dozens of hamburgers at his favorite restaurant daily, he would probably wind up morbidly obese. To blame the restaurant for his poor health, instead of his own personal indulgence, would be foolish and irresponsible.

When a person gives recreational drugs a try, ignoring the well-known promise of addiction, that is a very stupid decision on his part. When another spends all her income on fun, or extravagant clothing, or other non-necessities, that is definitely a badly thought-out choice. The time usually comes when she will complain that she is broke, homeless, and/or ill and wants someone else to bail her out of her predicament.

Folks, no doubt about it, we can be (and usually are) our own worst enemy. We impulsively decide to behave a certain way, or ingest a certain substance, or stuff our body with unhealthy food...and then we suffer the consequences. And just like that unfortunate and unthinking farmer, we alone bear the responsibility for our actions.

I think we would be wise to remember the words of that snake, "You knew I was a snake when you picked me up. I simply did what snakes do, I bit you." The snake wasn't responsible for the plight of the man. The man made a choice that led to being bit. The snake was only being what it is...a dangerous poisonous animal.

The Bible says that you will reap what you sow. People need to think a little more in-depth about what they are contemplating. Instead of impulsively acting, and then wanting to blame someone else for their problems when life implodes around them.

THE KING'S FOOL

The tale is told of a king who had a court jester on his staff. His job was to make the king laugh, to keep him in good humor and feeling like everything was okay. And this man did his job very well.

The time came when the country fell into hard economic years, and a depression settled on the people across the land. The king decided he needed to fix this problem, so he proclaimed the jester as "The King's Fool." He gave The King's Fool a golden scepter to represent his new title, and then instructed him to tour the kingdom for an extended time, making the people laugh. He was told to return to the throne room at the end of his long trip, to give his report to the old king.

After a long and discouraging journey throughout a famine-ridden land, the jester eventually returned to the king's lofty castle, where he appeared in front of the king to make his report. He proceeded to tell the old king just exactly what that foolish man wanted to hear. "Everything is wonderful in your kingdom, Your Majesty. Everyone is happy and laughing. And there is plenty of food for everyone."

But the old king didn't react the way the jester expected. He simply wasn't interested in how his people had been encouraged by the laughter and jokes of The King's Fool. In fact, he wasn't interested in anything, anymore. The sick and aging ruler finally admitted to the jester that he was dying.

"I am going on a long journey for which I am not prepared. I'm not sure where I will be going, and I am not certain if I shall ever return."

The jester replied in astonishment, "You are going on a journey, uncertain of your destination, not sure of its length, and you have made no preparation?"

"Yes," the feeble old king replied sadly.

The jester then handed his scepter to the king and said, "You, sire, are the greatest fool I have ever known. This truly belongs with you."

Death is certain. Are you prepared?

Ever sit and take the time to read through the OBITUARIES section of your local paper? Men and women who have recently died are memorialized in a short article that details their date of birth, death, family members, and their accomplishments. So many differences. But there is one thing they all have in common. They all lived…and they all died. Now, that observation may appear rather obvious, fearful, tragic, or even morbid to you. However, you must admit it is true. I once heard of a fellow recently who commented, "If I die…" to which his friend interrupted him to declare, "Oh, there is no "if" about it, my friend, you will die someday."

Scripture says we will all die, (Hebrews 9:27) and the only difference between any of us, is whether we are ready to meet our Lord and Creator.

THEY...ALMOST...WON THE GAME

During a recent NFL game, the offensive team drove to the opponent's one yard line and was preparing to score. Trailing by just five points, they only needed this touchdown to win, as there was only a second left in the game.

But then a grievous error was committed by that team, and sure enough, out came the dreaded referee's whistle. The problem? Delay of game! They had taken too much time to start the play that would have won them the game. The penalty? They were moved five yards further away from the goal line. When they finally executed their last play, the other team stopped them at that one-yard line, just one yard short of their intended goal.

Just three lousy little feet short of winning.

Now, let me explain a little more about this team. They had played a wonderful game. They had fought hard and faithfully to get within only five points of the other team at the end of the game. In the first fifty-nine plus minutes of that sixty-minute contest, they had executed well. But, in the very last few seconds, they caused themselves to lose everything they had worked so hard to achieve.

Thinking back on the game, I re-visited the foolishness of that game delay. And I suddenly realized it was much like so many people today. Folks can start out in life with good intentions and solid workable plans. They surround themselves with like-minded teammates and co-workers, and together they fight long and hard to achieve their goal. But somewhere along the years, they somehow begin to think they have plenty of time, and they end up getting side tracked from their goal. Causing themselves to get delayed…and that can create costly penalties.

Folks, we all seem to feel there is plenty of time, but in reality, there is not. I don't think that anyone plans to settle on anything less than their intended goals of success. And they don't set a lofty goal of, "My final home will certainly not be Heaven." But Scripture says, "Life is as a sigh." Meaning that life rushes by, seemingly quicker than a person breathes a sigh. Ask an elderly friend who has lived this truth. They will tell you, that in a lot of ways childhood seems like just yesterday.

The stark truth is this: You do not have any idea when that last heartbeat will happen. You cannot afford to delay anything that is important to you, because it can suddenly be too late. Eternally.

If you want to mend a relationship that is broken – pick up the phone. Get in your car. Send a text. But don't put it off. If you hope to make proper plans for eternity – do it now. That is one decision you do not want to put off. If you seek to change your habits, your lifestyle, or your career plans…do it now. Because delay may penalize you from realizing your greatest dreams.

The football team I spoke about? They had no one to blame but themselves. They had great plans, but took too long to act on them. The Bible says, "Boast not thyself of tomorrow, as tomorrow is promised to no man."

STUPID EXPECTS CHANGE – BUT WITH NO CHANGES

It is not an intelligent idea to ignore pain. If you have pain, or had pain in the recent past – physically, mentally, emotionally, maritally, financially, or any other '-ally,' there is a reason. Be smart and deal with it.

Readers, ARE YOU LISTENING TO WHAT YOU ARE READING? Please take all this to heart.

Pain is part of God's Warning System that something is beginning to malfunction and will most likely worsen if it is ignored. Don't make the mistake of being too busy to think about it. Too proud to try to make changes. Too scared of what you might be told if you go to a professional. And if you have already been given a diagnosis and have been told what needs to be done to prevent worsening future problems – don't ignore the advice. Make the changes needed. In whatever area that is hurting.

Because it is very unlikely that the problem will just magically go away. To the contrary, pain ignored is simply an invitation from you to that existing problem, "Go ahead, take over an even bigger part of my life and make yourself at home! In fact, you can live here as long as you want, I won't do a thing about it."

And if you have only just begun to glimpse faint flashes of a warning light that something is wrong in your life, don't be foolish and wait for the real pain to hit. Be smart. Get ahead of it. Investigate and try to get a jump on whatever has begun to say, "I'm almost completely thru your door, and when I do, you better believe that I'm gonna make my presence known, and I'm here to stay for a while."

Painful issues of any kind usually require making some adjustments, a different approach to living. Some examples; Your hurting marriage won't likely heal with simply the passing of time. A physical problem most usually doesn't just disappear on its own with no attention from you. Your empty bank account probably won't recover unless you adjust your spending habits. And if it is depression or an anger issue that is nagging at you, it has roots that rarely disintegrate alone.

I'll write it again. If you have pain, or had pain in the recent past – physically, mentally, emotionally, maritally, financially, or any other '-ally,' there is a reason. And it is not a smart idea to ignore that reason.

Interestingly, the expansion of that word, 'ignore' is the word 'ignorance.' And either meaning of that word ignorance, whether used as 'innocently unknowing' or as 'willfully and stupidly turning your back' means you probably stand to get hurt in the long run, either way.

V

KIDS: YOU SAID YOU WANTED THEM...

BEWARE: HELLION ALERT

The preschool–aged boy suddenly screamed like Beelzebub himself was after him.

Recently I was having a quiet lunch by myself in a local restaurant. The place was pleasantly filled with patrons, all quietly talking with companions at their individual tables and enjoying their lunch.

Then it happened!

The whole scene changed when "they" came through the door. Two young mothers entered, each with a small preschool child in tow. They were seated by the hostess across the room from where I sat. I already knew the little boy and his mother personally, having seen the child interact with his age group in church before – and knew him to be fairly quiet and well-behaved.

But no more than thirty seconds after being seated, that boy screamed like Beelzebub himself was after him. My head automatically jerked up in his direction, as did everyone else in the restaurant, ready to fight to defend this young child against whomever was threatening his life.

But there was no problem to be seen. He only wanted a drink – and he wanted it NOW! Evidently not getting his problem attended to quickly enough, he slapped his mother and let out another blood-curdling scream. This went on several times in the next few minutes, while I, along with all the other diners, scrambled to cram what remained of my lunch into my mouth, to get away from there. Even the employees seemed to be avoiding the area of this awful child.

What did his mom do? Nothing! She never changed her expression, but just continued her conversation with her friend. The whole time the child was screaming and terrorizing the room, his mom calmly plied him with whatever he was wanting; simply ignoring the fact that he was destroying lunchtime for a roomful of other diners. Never once telling him no, never once attempting to discipline a very unruly and untaught child.

Now, let it be known, I love children - and I love moms with children. But what I dislike and cannot abide is a little hellion, who is allowed to disrupt everyone around them. And I detest when the parents obviously are not being responsible to lovingly discipline and train their child. Folks, no one enjoys being around your adorable little one when your cutey is acting like a hellion.

The Bible is replete with scripture about "raising up children as they should go…" and about "a child left to themselves brings his mother to shame." When people are around your little one and end up leaving the area to avoid the loud, boisterous and uncontrolled behavior, remember the fault lies with you as the parent who has been unwilling to train your child. Not your child.

The only humorous thing in that whole scenario was the response of the other preschooler. Every time the boy would scream and slap his mother, this little girl had a look of shock and dismay on her face. I saw her glance upward at her mom, her tiny mouth wide open in disbelief. She acted like she couldn't believe what she was witnessing, she evidently didn't get away with such shocking behavior!

The Scripture says, "Whom the Lord loves He disciplines…" Might want to remember, Moms and Dads, this also applies to us parents when we aren't doing our jobs.

ONE MO' TIME!

When our first grandchild, Bailey Ann, was a preschooler, she often would spend time at our home, running and playing and having a great time. If you are a grandparent or any relative of a toddler, and you have the opportunity to spend time playing with them, you know how special that time truly is.

On one occasion, she ran through the living room, daring Andy to play chase and grab. She loved tussling and roughhousing with her Pappa. So, as she raced by he caught her up into his arms and swung her around. She immediately feigned offense and shouted, "Put me down!" He then carried her over to the couch and dropped her from as high as he could onto the cushions, which bounced her light little body up into the air. She landed laughing uncontrollably and scrambled up yelling, "One mo time, Pappa, one mo time!"

So he obliged, repeatedly tossing her into the air, her laughing her little head off and yelling "One mo' time!" They played this game over and over until Pappa wore out. Now some twenty years later, her childish laughter and that sweet baby voice crying out, "One mo' time, Pappa!" still rings in our memories.

Yes, years later we remember those days, and so does she. Not only does she remember all those fun times, but she remembers the feelings of love and security that came with those years surrounded by her family. She recalls that as a little girl, she knew "Everything is good in my world. I am loved and protected."

Folks, it is vitally important that parents, grandparents and loved ones work to create a peaceful sanctuary for little ones. Childhood is the foundation that every adult builds their life upon. And when they grow older and face the inevitable heartaches out in the real world, they need that concrete footing of childhood security.

No, having a wonderfully loving and stable childhood doesn't automatically guarantee a hope-filled, happy life as an adult. There is nothing on this earth that can do that. But we can all agree that a concrete foundation under a house sure gives that house a lot better chance of surviving the storms that always come.

But, what do we do, when the storms of heartache have already hit that child? When the underpinnings have already been knocked sideways?

If you live close by, then be there in every way you can. Love and caring are expressed by being actually present in their life, showing them that they truly matter to you. And remember to pray for them every day. Asking God to do what only He can do.

But if yours is a long-distance relationship, then it is the same for you. Pray for that child. Be present in their lives by long-distance contact. Phone calls, texts, e-mails, cards and letters…whatever means you have. Let them know that you are interested in them, and whatever is important to them is important to you. Let them know they are loved and special to you.

Can you single-handedly fix their heartaches and problems with your love and attention? Wipe away all their pain? No. But you can let them know they're not alone. Assure them that they are loved and that you care. And to a child, or to a grownup, that may mean the difference between giving up and keeping their hope alive.

KIDS LOVE THE TRASH

They were just two toddlers, barely out of babyhood. And their parents were so very young and broke, existing just above poverty status. But they loved their little boys, and when Christmas time rolled around that year, they did their very best to provide a few new toys and much-needed new clothes for their rambunctious sons.

Early Christmas morning in their small living room found the two little boys happily opening their gaily wrapped boxes. The gift-giving had been short-lived, due to the few boxes under the little tree. But not ever accustomed to having an over-abundance of possessions, they were content and in high spirits over their new bounty.

Soon Mom and Dad stepped out of the living room to get dressed for the rest of the day. From their room of the small two-bedroom home, it was easy to hear the giggling comments of their little sons as they explored their new toys, so they knew they would be safely entertained for several minutes.

Dad returned to the living room scene a few minutes later, expecting to see his three-year-old son pushing his new toy truck along the forewarned and forbidden surface of the coffee table. Instead, he stopped in the doorway in surprise. Those boys were not happily involved with their new toys. They were laughing as they crawled in and out of the discarded boxes and wrapping paper…all the long-anticipated toys left abandoned somewhere on the floor under the Christmas trash.

Later that day recounting the incident to Grandma, the dad shook his head at the irony. "I could have saved so much money by getting them a bunch of huge empty boxes and stuffing them with used wrapping paper! They were having so much fun crawling in and out of that mess!"

Yes, we were the young parents in that tale from long ago. Some days later, ironically a local news report reminded us of our babies choosing to play with the trash instead of their toys. We sat listening to the reporter recount how some folks were living a sad sordid time in their lives, abusing and destroying themselves, and each other. Playing with trash instead of treasuring their gifts.

Folks, your God gave you the wonderful gift of relationships you have with your family. And yet so many make the mistake of abusing and taking their family for granted. They cheapen the gift they have been given by making hurtful comments to their loved one, and in some cases, even physically battering them, causing even more pain.

Scripture teaches that children are a gift from God. But many are neglected, abused, and tossed aside while their parents are caught up with what are "more important things in their life." That is throwing away the gifts given to you by God, and deliberately choosing to play with the trash instead.

Remember the old saying. "Keep the main thing the main thing." Determine to do things right from now on. Treasure God's gifts to you and put the trash out of your life.

ARE THE BABY CRADLES ROCKED ANYMORE?

The pastor had just concluded his message on the modern family. His final statement expressed his hope and prayer, "That the children in today's world will all be able to live in a sweet and godly home." At the end of the service, families flooded the aisles and headed to their vehicles to leave.

One particular family piled into their car, fastened their seatbelts, and prepared to get in line with all the other churchgoers to exit the parking lot. Suddenly, from his seat in the back, four-year-old Richie could be heard beginning to sniffle. As the sniffling quickly turned into sobs and showed no signs of quitting, Dad pulled out of the exit line, stopped the car and turned around in his seat to face the child. His irritation at the interruption was evident on his face and in his voice as he asked the boy why he was so upset.

Little Richie looked up, tears streaming, and hiccupped his way thru his explanation. "Pastor Johnson said, hic, he wants all us kids to live in a sweet and godly home, hic, but Daddy, I wanna live with you guys!"

Humorous…oh yeah. Timely…ouch. Could a variation of this little drama play out in homes across our nation on a regular basis, every time a pastor dares to speak out on the enormous problems in our families today?

A church family can put on a good front for the pastor and other church folks on Sunday morning, but the family members know what truly goes on behind closed doors at home. They hear the fights, the cold silences, the misunderstandings that are allowed to escalate into full-scale wars. The kids may have grown accustomed to what they hear, but believe me, that doesn't mean they enjoy it.

What do children see and hear at home? Are family dinners enjoyable, (if they actually happen at all) a time when mom and dad and the kids like to be together? Or is dinner just a time of slicing and dicing each other? Do family members at the table offer emotional support to each other, or is it just a perfect time to land a great crippling verbal hit? Mom and Dad, they need to sense love, security, and kindness, because as we all know, the world gives them a steady diet of anger, rejection and pain. They don't need more at home.

The first group God organized when He created the earth was the Family. It is considered to be the first church, and God intended it to be a place of security – a haven of love, encouragement and support. Many of us know scripture about "Children, obey your parents," but we overlook the verses that say, "Fathers, provoke not your children to anger," "Wives, give reverence and honor to your husband" and "Husbands, love your wives as you love yourself."

Folks, if we do not begin to shore up our family units, then our culture and our nation will continue this severe downhill slide. Because after all; as the family goes, so goes the country. As Abraham Lincoln was quoted, "The hand that rocks the cradle rules the world."

Take the time to love as God loves you. Take the time to rock the cradle.

FAIL OR SUCCEED, BUT LET THEM CHOOSE THEIR PATH

You have seen it, surely. The tomboy mom who somehow gave birth to a princess daughter who despises the dirty outdoors, and instead loves makeup and high fashion. Leaving the mother to wonder if two babies got swapped in the hospital. Confusing stuff to moms, sometimes.

Andy was a farm boy and truly loves that lifestyle. But he always pastored churches located in small towns, so our two sons were not raised in a farm atmosphere. In adulthood, both became city-preferring men. Sounds reasonable, given their town upbringing.

But now one grown son has a boy who has lived in a large city all his life and has no desire to continue that lifestyle. That kid is an outdoor-loving, "in-my-blood" pig farmer. Whether it is a humid sweltering Oklahoma summer day, or the brass monkey is knocking frantically on his front door, this teen enjoys the feeding, watering and the care of his pigs. Even volunteers to help his friends with their pig chores.

Education-oriented Mom and police officer Dad encourage him and help all they can – given that raising smelly pigs is not their calling in life. Why? Besides the fact that they love him, they recognize the wisdom of Proverbs 22:6, "Train up a child in the way he should go and when he is old, he will not depart from it." This scripture is not saying to train up your child in the way YOU think he should go. But rather, train the child in the way that individual child should go.

Don't make the mistake of pigeonholing your child into your ideas and beliefs. You may have recognized personality traits and intellect in your little girl that would make an excellent doctor, but let her follow her own inclinations.

And it is also not saying a child will never stray or fail. Failure and confusion go with the territory of growing up. Mistakes will happen, and even occasional mutiny may break out. Teens naturally have a rebellious streak inside, combined with a brain that will not fully mature until their early twenties. Keep this combination in mind, as they are driving you crazy while they are trying to break free from childhood and become an adult.

The word stressful doesn't seem to do justice for this time in their life…and everyone around them. Anybody who has been in the vicinity of a teenager for five minutes can agree. But is it possible that there could be a little less push-back and rebellion if a teenager was given firm boundaries of guidance, and then was allowed to find himself inside those protective fences?

Imagine a free-spirited wild pony forever locked up in a small paddock. Or the made-to-soar eagle forced to walk on the ground with turkeys. Imagine the friendly, loving labrador retriever that is given the lonely job of guarding the bank vault. Real possibility of rebellion in all those scenarios also.

What the Bible is saying is this: "A child may fumble and struggle while finding his niche. Patiently help him, don't bully him. And when he is finally an adult, he will find his world." Every baby arrives with inborn tendencies, desire and gifts. The job of the parent is to set godly boundaries, and to be your child's cheerleader as The Search begins.

Raising kids is hard…don't make it harder.

DON'T LEAVE YOUR KIDS THE LEGACY OF LIMPING

We all want to succeed at working, thinking, and being loved, but some just seem born to have a greater ability to do these things. You've seen it. The naturally handsome, smart and talented football quarterback. Or the lady who has it all - money, beauty and brains. While the rest of us struggle along with what we manage to scrape together.

Seems pretty unfair, doesn't it? But just how does this bald-faced blatant injustice happen? How did those people get it all, and the rest of us are stuck with being just "me?'

Much of it comes from a thing called family legacy. The things inherited from the generations before.

But I am not just referring to the legacy of inherited money, or inherited beauty traits. This legacy is the emotional climate of your childhood home. A security and confidence that comes from stability. Giving you the confidence that you can attempt anything and fail, and it's still okay. That is why having Mom, Dad, and grandparents involved in a child's life is so invaluable.

Without emotional stability from a child's family, there is a hole left in the heart that no amount of money or beauty can fill. And that hole negatively influences their confidence in decision-making, finding a mate who understands how to love and be loved, and their ability to live well. Or otherwise. For the rest of their life.

Don't misunderstand, there have been many who have worked and successfully overcame this heart-hole. But that is my point. It takes enormous work to overcome. Work that the emotionally secure in life do not have to struggle to do.

Outside appearances can be very deceiving. Talk with a child in a very wealthy family, but whose parents rarely schedule family time. You will hear the sad results. Always having the best that money can buy never replaces what money can't buy.

Now look at the other side of the coin. Talk to the one who had the privilege of being reared in a family where family time, unconditional love, discipline and open honesty was just part of life. You will hear an adult who had a leg up on contemporaries from the very beginning. Because no matter what may happen in the coming years, good or bad, that blessed child had an immovable mountain of granite at his or her back... the legacy of stability.

So, here is the question. How to change the course of an unfortunate family legacy?

Begin learning what you were never taught. Put your Creator first – living the way He designed for his creation. Get in a good church and spend time with families - rich or poor - who model a healthy emotional climate. Deliberately create the time to emotionally invest in your child. Love and forgive your mate for any pain of the past, so that you can stay together.

Bottom line. Kids thrive on emotional stability. They become emotionally healthy adults who can run - instead of limping through life.

TINY TYRANT NEVER BEEN SPANKED... AND IT SHOWS

You can see a lot standing in the checkout line at Walmart.

Waiting patiently for your turn, your mind occupied while you run through your to-do list for the rest of the day, you are abruptly jolted back into reality by a preschooler.

A four-year-old boy directly in line in front of you has decided he desperately needs a candy bar...now. His mom, baby in one arm and a basket of groceries hanging on the other, quietly explains to Tommy that the lack of sugar right then is not going to ruin his life.

Telling him he can have a candy bar later; she tries to engage him in a detailed conversation regarding why this was not the time. She might have as well been promising him sauerkraut buried in a bowl of mushy broccoli from the response she receives. As she talks, he completely ignores her while repeatedly slamming the candy up on the conveyor belt. Only to have her quietly remove it each time.

Then the whining starts while the slamming and removing continues. Mom sweetly telling him why she was not buying it for him. By this time, she is standing in front of the cashier who is waiting for payment. The line behind her is getting longer, her son's whining is getting louder, the baby in her arms has begun fussing, and the cashier is obviously frustrated. (No doubt in my mind, this little Hitler knows he has Mom over a barrel and it would be only a matter of time until he wins.) But still, Mom keeps leaning down, sweetly attempting to reason with Tommy the Tyrant.

Then it happened. Right there, in front of God, the cashier, and everybody in that line, Tommy suddenly shrieked and slapped Mom in the face. And then something else happened. I leaned forward and kindly offered to hold her fussing baby, so she could take care of business and give that tyrannical toddler the spanking he needed.

Yeah, I did.

I really thought that would be better than offering to do it for her.

By her reaction, you would have thought I was the one who had slapped her. Horrified, she snarled, "SPANK MY SON? I have never!" To which the cashier muttered, "Yeah, we all can tell that!" Mom angrily grabbed her sweet darling boy and left the store in a huff...to the sound of applause from all the shoppers who had been stuck in the line behind her.

Folks, in Proverbs 29:15, Scripture tells us that children left to themselves bring their mothers to shame. Implied is the advice; love your young ones enough to teach and discipline them. Shape their behavior while you can. You are not loving them by ignoring that part of their childhood - you are hurting them. Most people actually do love children, but they have little tolerance for out-of-control kids.

Me, too.

CHRISTMASTIME WITH DAD

Back when Andy was a child with four siblings, Christmas time was a huge deal in their home. Those kids planned, shopped the catalogues, and hung onto the words of every loud and colorful Christmas commercial that came on television. Dreaming of the BIG DAY that seemed to take forever to arrive.

But as much as the kids longed for Christmas, their own excitement couldn't hold a candle to that of their dad. He had grown up in a modest-income family during the middle of the Great Depression, and while the holiday was still observed, it had to be in a very minimal way. So, I am guessing that getting to experience Christmas gift giving thru the eyes of his children was a tremendous thrill to him.

Andy can remember his dad looking thru the toy catalogs with all five of his children, taking the time to listen and comment on all of their "I want this one!" or, "This is it, right here!" and "That one is gonna be mine!" Dad would tease them about being good and what Santa would bring to nice little boys and girls.

During that holiday season, he invariably would bring home an assortment of candies. Hard candies in bright colors were a staple throughout those days of

December. Sugary orange slices and chocolate drops are indelibly seared into Andy's memories of childhood Christmases.

Many years later, his mom told them that Dad would always manage to arrange his work schedule to be home on Christmas Eve, even though he worked the graveyard shift for twenty-plus years. On Christmas Eve, he would insist that the kids had to go to bed early, so Santa would come. Then they would lie there wide awake for what seemed like hours, listening to the quiet clinking of toy construction. Andy can still recall as a small boy hearing noise on the roof of their home that night. And being totally convinced the next morning (with Dad's help) that it must have been Santa Claus that he heard.

On Christmas morning, his dad could hardly wait for the kids to wake up. In later years, his mom laughingly admitted that he would begin around 2:30 or 3:00, asking her if it wasn't time for the kids to get up. Usually by 4:30, or 5:00 at the latest, he "thought" he heard one of them rousing, and would feel that all the others needed to wake up. Then Christmas morning would begin, with all the confusion, excitement and noise level that five young kids can generate in one small living room.

The kids were always thrilled with whatever Santa brought, but no one was more pleased than Dad himself. Every year, holding the same green cup filled with hot coffee, he would play with each child. He would check out every new dress, toy truck and popgun with the greatest of interest. Andy can still vividly recall seeing him tenderly rocking the youngest sister's new baby doll, as he talked with her about the needs of her new dolly. Surely, no one had a better Christmas morning than Andy's dad. His excitement, his anticipation, his joy.

Now, let's get real here. Was it plausible that this grown man was enthralled with toy guns? Do we really believe this adult male with five children loved rocking an artificial baby in his arms while speculating about its care? Nah, that was simply a father who loved his kids enough to play-act for their benefit. He loved seeing the happiness on their faces, and probably would have been willing to juggle knives while standing on his head if that would have been necessary.

Oh, that every dad would decide to experience that kind of exuberance for living life and loving their families. That every dad would own his version of a green coffee cup that his adult kids will remember all their life.

VI

BECOMING A GROWN UP: GRIT YOUR TEETH AND BEAR IT

THINGS ARE NOT ALWAYS AS THEY APPEAR

Tom lived in Smallsville. Everybody knew each other, and they all knew each other's routines and habits. Tom had grown up in that town, and all the citizens of Smallsville knew of Tom's rough and reckless lifestyle. Since his teen years, his old red Ford truck could be found in front of one of the bars in town every weekend.

But one day Tom finally recognized his probable future, by looking over his shoulder at his past. Making his decision, right then and there he asked God to help him make a change. He became an active and faithful member of a local church, serving and helping others wherever he could.

Folks definitely saw and enjoyed a new Tom in their town.

However, one evening he was summoned to meet with the pastor and a group of the church's leaders. The purpose of the gathering was soon made clear when Widow Johnson cleared her throat and crossed her arms over her chest. Through tightly pursed lips, she began addressing the group.

Seems the night before, she had witnessed Tom's old Ford truck parked out in front of his former favorite local watering hole for an extended period of time. "He must have spent the entire evening drinking at that bar, because with my own two eyes, I saw his truck parked out front for hours," she stated vehemently. Glaring coldly at the offender, she then declared him backslidden and in need of church discipline.

The wise old pastor slowly turned to face Tom. Taking a deep calming breath, he asked the young man if he would like to speak on his own behalf and give an explanation that would clear this up. They all listened as Tom patiently explained that his truck had broken down on the way home from work and he had coasted to a halt – admittedly stopping in front of the bar. By the time he had been able to get it towed, his truck had indeed been in that parking lot for hours.

Despite his explanation of the facts, Mrs. Johnson still adamantly believed what she had seen with her own two eyes. The rest of the group agreed that prayer seemed to be the only answer for Tom and Mrs. Johnson. The meeting was adjourned after Tom assured them that he would definitely be aware and careful where he parked from now on.

Indeed, that night Tom was very deliberate where he parked before walking on home to his house. Tongues began wagging early the next morning, as Smallsville woke up to see Tom's red truck parked in front of Widow Johnson's house.

Ouch. Oh, my.

As Widow Johnson discovered to her dismay, just because you saw or heard something doesn't make it an actual fact. "That's exactly what I saw," or "That's precisely what I heard" can sometimes create conclusions that are based on assumption. And even if it is fact, nothing good comes from passing along gossip that is hurtful. As grandpa said years ago, "God shore enuff gave us two ears and one mouth, so maybe we ought'ta listen twice as much as we talk."

OWN IT... IT'S YOURS

You actually did it.

You won the election. Or in the last second, you sunk the shot that won the game. Or your business was named in the top ten gor growth in your category. Maybe, you actually got ol' Ms. Fussbudget to laugh during English class. Or just maybe, you lost the weight that has plagued you for so long.

Whatever it was that you did – own it. It came from you, and it was your own success. No one else can claim that they did what was clearly your accomplishment. There is no need for you to hang your head and deny that you succeeded. No need for you to declare that it was really someone else. Yes absolutely, thank those who helped you or guided you, and give them the acknowledgement that they deserve. But never back away from realizing and accepting that it could not have happened apart from your own decisions, desire, and work.

Feels good, doesn't it? To hold your head high and give yourself a pat on the back for succeeding. To accept that you "did good." That you are not aways making a mistake or not trying hard enough to be a winner. In doing so, you are setting yourself up to see yourself in a good light – and that does make a person feel good. It will probably make you want to try even harder to win the next time.

But let me flip that proverbial pancake to the other side.

You made a major mistake, or you gave up trying and just walked away without a word. No one else is to blame. And there isn't a valid excuse for what occurred…. simply that you were wrong. And a really big error was the result.

You. Just. Goofed.

What then?

Accept it, own it. It was your mistake, not someone else around you. To attempt to lay blame on anyone else accomplishes a lot…and none of it good. Namely, you won't learn to take responsibility for your own problems, and secondly, that person you are blaming will resent you for a long time. Doesn't do much for your relationship with them.

Another fact to consider; those around you who already know the real truth – or they find out later – will see you differently, and not in a good way. (And the Bible says the truth will always come out sooner or later. Numbers 32:23)

It's best to just honestly examine what happened– openly and clearly. Look closely at your own actions, motivations and conversations. If what you find makes you squirm, then own it. Sure, there is usually always someone's behavior you can factor in to make you feel better about it all. But that doesn't change what you did. Just own it, and try to make amends the best you can.

And then forgive yourself. Because NOTHING good comes from living in guilt and shame. Because, we usually behave according to how we feel about ourselves.

LOOK AT THAT ONE WITH THE LIMP AND THE BANDAGE

We all see them, at Wal Mart, the workplace, or looking in the mirror. Maybe with a sling on their arm, or favoring a strained back muscle, or limping through the door on their good leg.

Bar fight? Strong disagreement with their spouse? Exercise workout gone south? Good chance it's none of those possibilities. Probably the result of an old-fashioned thing called Weekend Warrior On The Warpath.

"I only have this Saturday and Sunday to build a treehouse for my kids." Or, "Weatherman says it's supposed to start raining early Monday morning, so I gotta get my whole garden tilled up, and planted this weekend."

Something backbreaking along those lines, anyway.

Or maybe you're one of those who takes a good, long, honest look in your full-length mirror and decides that this will be the weekend you completely remove those extra twenty-five pounds. Don't be surprised if you get acquainted with your local ER personnel, or at the very least spend a lot of time in the company of your mattress.

Cram a physical activity your body hasn't done in months into one furiously-paced weekend, and you're likely to find your muscles rebelling and accidents happening. Most likely you will recover, your tired and strained muscles will rest and heal. Slowly. And if you didn't get your Warrior Goal finished before you fell over in pain, you will probably be feeling like getting back to it the next weekend. Maybe.

Good for you. Don't give up, just get a little smarter about it. Realize you are older this year than you were 365 days ago, and that does make a difference. Make some adjustments to your goal of how much weight you can lose in only forty-eight hours and you'll be fine. Accept the possibility that you may have to take more than one weekend to finish that playhouse or your garden – nothing to beat yourself up about. Just do it at a reasonable pace for you.

Oh, yeah, there'll probably be bruises, even if you take your time on your self-assignment. But bruises turn purple, then blue, then an ugly yellow, and go away. Don't be afraid of the bruises, be more afraid of not trying to accomplish your goal.

Life is something we need to enjoy, to live the best we can. A time to involve yourself in whatever activity that brings a smile to your face – albeit maybe just before the grimace of pain. Go ahead and get busy with your plans, maybe just learn to tailor those plans a little.

Join that softball league, plant that garden, toss a softball with the neighbor kid in the yard you slowly raked yesterday. You don't have to do it perfectly, and you don't have to get it done in a certain amount of time. Just get started in the doing. Don't vegetate on your sofa, find what you like to do and do it.

HAMMERS, PIGS, AND COWS CAN MAKE A FARMER CUSS

Andy has always said that his dad, whom I never had the privilege of meeting, was a fairly mild-mannered easy-going guy. Respected and well-liked in his rural community, a boys' baseball coach, and a church-goer – seems he had a friendly word for everyone. Even when riled, he wasn't a man to easily lose control of his temper. Like everyone, he had one, but he just usually kept it pretty well under.

Except.

From listening to the family telling stories of yesteryear, there were two things in life that made that man lose his grip; one was cows and pigs that refused to cooperate when they were being loaded into the chute. And the other that lit his fuse? Hitting his thumb with a badly-aimed hammer blow.

From what I understand, a stubborn Bossy The Cow, or Pearl The Pig could suddenly become the recipient of very imaginative names not normally given to four-legged animals. And on fence-building days? The air on their farm would take on a whole new shade of blue when his dad splattered his thumb at that task. Then his kids would spend the next half-hour searching for his hammer. Eventually finding it in the neighbor's pasture.

Sound kinda familiar? You may not be a hammer-wielding farmer with bad aim and five kids snickering when you miss. And you may not be the proud owner of panicked pigs and cows that suddenly have their own ideas when it comes to being loaded up and taken to the slaughter house.

But you probably are the owner of a temper. Whether it reminds people of instantly combustible Fire From Hell Itself, or slow simmering Volcanic Lava, you most likely possess one. Seems to be part of being a human being. I have never met anyone yet who absolutely never has a flareup of that 'thing' inside of us, that attitude that lets those around us know we are not a happy camper.

But maybe, you actually are known worldwide as Calm Calvin or Sweetheart Sara. You are one of those rare species who never shows any anger or disgust, and never disagrees with anyone. Then I would venture to guess you may privately deal with things like tension headaches, upset stomach, sudden diarrhea, or stomach ulcers. Not a good trade-off.

Better plan? Learn to express your displeasure, (without a missing hammer) listen to the opposing opinion if there is any, create a workable solution, ask and give forgiveness when needed, and then move on.

Life is way-y-y-y-y-y too hard to spend your time holding your negative emotions in so tightly that you become ill. You will eventually find yourself spending a portion of your time dealing with that illness, instead of just simply living openly and honestly. Learn to feel it, express it, and deal with it.

But just remember, everyone else is dealing with difficult emotions and situations too. So let's cut each other some slack.

IF IT'S ALREADY BAD NEWS, DON'T MAKE IT WORSE

Ever been caught in a situation where your say-so doesn't carry enough weight to hold a feather down? When you totally disagree with the decision or coming results, but there isn't much you can do to change what's coming? I can hear the resounding 'Oh Yeah!' from every reader.

So, what do you do? Yell obscenities, throw stuff at the TV, fall to the floor in a full-fledged childish tantrum? Complain loudly and bitterly to any and every person within earshot? Could be. I don't know how you react to unpleasant news. But if that is your modus operandi, does it do any good – change anything?

Consider this true story.

As a twenty-year-old inexperienced untrained preacher, Andy accepted his first pastoral position. He and his expectant wife, Renie, relocated from the city to an isolated area of the Oklahoma Panhandle so he could assume his very first pastorate. Andy quickly realized that his greatest supporter in that tiny church was Deacon Cook. Faithful, prayer warrior, and encourager, this godly man was there for his pastor in every way he could.

About a year later, Pastor Andy's family was in the Cook home for Sunday lunch. During the pre-meal conversation that deacon commented, "Preacher, when we voted to ask you to be our pastor, you never requested to see the vote totals. Why?"

Rather sheepishly Andy replied, "Guess because I didn't know I was supposed to ask." (He has since learned otherwise.) With a kind smile Deacon Cook then told him, "Well, the vote that day was 14-9, in favor of calling you to come."

"Not a very positive vote, huh?" a rather embarrassed Andy answered.

Tears flooded that deacon's eyes as he admitted, "Preacher, I voted against you. And I am sure sorry I did. I realized later that I was wrong."

Amazing.

Up until then, Andy never had an inkling that deacon had voted against him. Quite the contrary, Deacon Cook had always been encouraging, loving, and supportive. A mentor who helped build him into a better leader and minister. The opposite could have happened. Had that man turned into a bitter and angry deacon, he could have created problems for that inexperienced pastor. And that little church would have suffered. But instead, he chose the high road, exhibiting respect and encouragement. Even in the face of woefully untried leadership.

Even when we know we are right in our thinking; if we aren't careful, we can be wrong in our actions. And make things much worse if we do. Deacon Cook had a godlier way of handling disappointment and controversy. And saved a church from a lot of heartache.

Not very much change occurs in a man's heart, when a sworn enemy demands that change. To the contrary, many times stubbornness takes over on both sides and noses get out of joint. Much more effective in the long-run? Be as supportive as possible, try calm reasoning instead of angry confrontation, and pray constantly for our Creator to create a change of heart – on both sides.

A BLEEDING BOTTOM LIP IS BETTER THAN SMELLING SKUNKY

We've all had to be around them. Usually, everyone has one or more in the family tree – hopefully a good way away from your own particular branch. But even if you are fortunate enough to not be situated in close proximity to Cousin Crabby – you probably still get blowback from the family members who have no choice but to be around him. And you can easily spot those unlucky ones by the dazed, disgruntled, and depressed haze that occasionally surrounds them.

Who are these people that make others want to run and hide when they come around? The people that I am convinced inspired Caller ID? Who turn the very air around them a dark grimy gray when they enter the room? Perpetually angry and grouchy people. Those walking thunderstorms, who for whatever reason, have decided that their life has to be lived in a black mood. And that yours should be also, so it is their job to ensure that happens.

You can absolutely decide ahead of time, "When I have no choice but to take her phone call, I WILL NOT get sucked into that dark hole where Grumpy

Greta lives and wants everyone else to inhabit also. I absolutely refuse!" Then the phone rings, and the caller ID notifies you of impending gloom. You take a deep breath, pray for Almighty God to protect you, and then cheerfully answer. Only to hear a grim, deadly voice coming from a deep black hole in the middle of the earth, "I. AM. UNHAPPY."

Then the litany of woe begins assailing your bleeding ears. And no matter what you say in the next thirty-seven minutes and twenty-two seconds, it is wrong. There are no carefully worded suggestions that will be acceptable. No subtle, or otherwise, change of subject moves Grumpy from her firmly fixed focus – to make certain you are fully versed as to the reasons she has the worst life ever lived on this green earth.

And may God help your unfortunate misguided soul if you dare to disagree with this poor woman. One hint of the words, "But maybe…." and World War III threatens to submerge you over the air waves. It just isn't worth it. Better to grab your roll of duct tape and plaster it two inches deep across your mouth, than to bring down the Wrath of Kahn's cousin upon yourself. Just stay silent and tough it out until the onslaught is over. And while you are waiting for deliverance, just bite your bottom lip until your sacrificial blood drips onto your chin. While comforting yourself with thoughts of hot gooey cinnamon rolls and a cup of steaming coffee waiting on you in the kitchen.

An old man once put it this way, "Arguin' with folks who like fussin' and fightin' is like wrestlin' with a skunk. Both wind up smellin' bad, but the skunk likes it."

Remember this, when that person who makes you wish you could evaporate into thin air contacts you… don't bother arguing, 'cause a bleeding bottom lip is better than smelling like a skunk.

SEE AND BE: THAT IS A LIE

A man was put under for a medical procedure. When he awoke, he asked the nurse attending him, "Is it all over, am I okay?" She assured him that yes, it was over, he was just fine and all was well. He then said, "Oh, good. Tell me, will I be able to play the piano?" To which she replied, "Well, of course you will!" With a groggy impish grin came his answer, "Wow! I'm glad, 'cause I never could before!"

There seems to be a modern movement afoot that claims, 'If you see others doing it, and if you want, you can do it also.' See…be.

Oh, c'mon!

Wanting to do or be what God did not intend for your life, is a struggle that pits you against enormous odds. And for our children to be indoctrinated that they can be and do anything they choose, is a lie. They are unfairly being set up for a life filled with frustration and many times, failure.

A five-foot six-inch guy can spend years watching seven-foot-tall basketball players run up and down the court like gazelles and dunk the ball with six inches to spare. He can admire them, he can enviously want to be their height, he can even practice for the next ten years to be just like them – BUT HE CAN'T BE SEVEN FEET TALL!

To tell someone who is totally deaf that they can be a famous opera singer... probably not. A child who struggles enormously with the most basic math is not going to have an easy time becoming an astronaut. A baby born without legs is certainly going to struggle to become a fireman – no matter how strongly he wants to be one.

Don't read this column wrong. I am NOT saying to never encourage them to be the best, to never dream big. Kids need to be taught to set high goals and to pursue what they want, with everything within them. But the last four words of that sentence above is the key...with everything within them.

Inspire them to find the strengths that are built within them. Don't be the Cold-Water Committee, always telling them, "You really can't." On the contrary, encourage your children to try whatever they enjoy, but to pursue what they are truly gifted to be.

And according to the Bible, they are gifted by their Creator to do something in His plan.

The Apostle Peter asked Jesus, "What is John going to do?" To which Jesus responded, "What is that to you? *You do what I called you to do.*" (Italics are from this writer.)

Pursue dreams and goals, yes, but realize and accept reality. And then race madly toward a goal for which you have gifts and talents to accomplish. We can't just "See & Be." Not unless we have that gift and talent. But we can reach that goal we were made to reach.

Don't let an advertising campaign frustrate you or your kids. Tell them - and yourself - the real truth, so you can get busy doing what you can actually do.

NOW UNDERSTAND; I'M JUST TELLING YOU WHAT I HEARD

The church's youth leader played a lot of games with our church youth group. One simple game in particular stands out in memory. Maybe because it was fun, and maybe because it plainly showed impressionable young minds how people hurt people.

We would all stand in a circle, shoulder to shoulder. Our leader would then whisper a sentence into the ear of the teen standing next to him. He in turn would whisper what he heard into the ear of the person standing next to him, and so on. By the time the story got back to the originator, it had been, shall we say, "enhanced and embellished." The altered and expanded version resembled nothing of his original sentence.

Why did that happen? Because there was one rule; you could not ask any questions of the one who whispered in your ear. You could only turn to the next teen and repeat what you thought you heard. As a result, a sentence such as, "The white pig lay sleeping on the floor of the barn," would easily be heard as "The light pig lay sleeping on all four of the arms." Then that teen would look you as if you had just confirmed her long-held suspicions that you were an idiot. But she would shrug her shoulders, and turn to tell the next hearer and whisper something to the effect of, "The shy pig came sweeping in on four arms?"

Normally, it wasn't that someone simply decided to create havoc and distort the message deliberately. Sometimes that happened, but usually it was the result of the listener not completely understanding the sentence that was whispered to him. Every word wasn't caught clearly, and he was duty bound to pass on to the next player exactly what he thought he heard.

Yeah, I know, probably every one of you readers can recall playing this popular game at some point in your youth. Fun stuff for a group of teenagers. The game was called Gossip, and it was very effective at demonstrating to us why "I'm just telling you what I heard…" is so dangerous and damaging.

But unfortunately, this tired old game is still played today. But it's not a game, it is teens and adults doing what they do in real life. And in the process, they are hurting others and even ruining lives. Beloved readers, you must understand; in today's world, people would rather believe a lie than believe the truth. And juicier stuff makes it even better.

To make the problem even worse, today we have social media that people are using to pass on information – truth or outrageous lies. People of all ages are repeating what they were told, and their friends are accepting it, believing it and repeating it….and actually embellishing it as they continue to spread the poison. Rumors, innuendos, and outright lies are out there and are causing real harm.

Jesus taught in His Sermon on the Mount, "Let your communication be yea, yea, and nay, nay; for whatsoever is more than these, cometh of evil." Remember, what goes around in a circle comes around. You could be the next one to be hurt from the so-called harmless "…I'm just telling you what I heard."

DON'T PLANT PEAS AND EXPECT SPAGHETTI

While watching tv the other night, a commercial came on that got my attention. Yeah, that's right. Believe it or not, an ad that was worth watching. In a closeup of his face, the owner of a local business was speaking directly into the camera. And lo and behold, he was actually not pushing his product!

Instead, he was commenting about the escalating price of everything we buy. Then he made a statement that caught my attention. Without trying to quote him, here is the essence of what he said. "Everything is costing too dadgum much anymore. Food, housing, gasoline, cars. You name it - and chances are you probably can't afford it. But there is something that you and I can give away, and it costs absolutely nothing. Kindness, try it. Cause we all need it."

Try giving away a smile and an encouraging word to the tired grocery store worker next time you are buying eggs and milk that is costing you too much. Say a heartfelt "Thank you" to the air conditioner technician, who is working overtime to try to keep everyone cool in the heat of summer. Offer to laugh at yourself at work, instead of coating the whole area in criticism and negativity.

Be kind. It costs you nothing. In fact, you will harvest some benefits from it. Like the Bible says, you reap what you sow. True stuff. Any farmer will tell you that if you plant peas, don't be looking to harvest spaghetti. Peas planted and watered are going to give you more of exactly what you put into the ground. More peas.

So don't be spreading grouchiness and complaining, and then pray for crop failure. If you lay a round of cursing and yelling on the mechanic that is supposed to be fixing your vehicle by tomorrow – you probably shouldn't expect him to work hard to get your truck back to you ASAP. In fact, you just may get a text from him, "Parts not available for two weeks." Sorry, dude, but you brought it on yourself. Might try a little kindness and friendliness next go-round. Pea pods don't sprout spaghetti.

So, will being Little Miss Sunshine bring only roses and perfection into your life? You know better. Life is hard – the pits at times. And you are increasing the chances that it will be that way, when you are being disagreeable and grumpy to everyone around you day after day. Because life has a way of giving back to you exactly what you give out.

Try this. Deliberately try. Make life a little easier for those who are forced to be around you. It costs you nothing, and in time (when the shock wears off) they will probably start treating you with a lot more kindness and consideration.

Remember, peas planted make a bunch of peas…and only peas.

CHURCHESE IS A FOREIGN LANGUAGE

A little while back, Andy was a patient in the hospital of a major metropolitan city. It is highly rated in the medical world, and we both felt assured that he was in good hands. The doctors and nurses were professional, proficient and personable. He was well cared for, and they certainly knew their business.

But there was something else besides the outstanding level of expertise that we kept noticing. Much to our discomfort and anxiety.

These top-notch health-care providers seemed to originate from all over the world, guessing from the accents as they spoke English to us. Heavily foreign, it was sometimes very difficult to understand what they were saying. There was no doubt that they knew what they were talking about, being the trained professionals that they are, but we were struggling to keep up with the conversation. And as that conversation was about Andy's health, we certainly felt the need to keep up.

Seeing the confused look on Andy's face, one young nurse finally told us, "I talk too fast and I have a heavy accent that makes it hard to understand me. Please just slow me down and I will start again for you." I am guessing we were not the only ones to ever stand in front of her with a helplessly dumb look, as she tried to explain procedures.

Because of this experience, we have realized something more strongly than ever.

We Christians are used to speaking fluent 'Churchese' with each other. We are familiar with church terms and words, as that language is second nature to anyone who has been in worship services very much. Therefore, it never dawns on us that when we try to talk to non-church people about faith, that if we are not careful, they likely don't understand a lot of what we are saying. If it were me standing in their shoes and someone did that to me, I would likely feel very uncomfortable and intimidated. Not a good scenario.

You and I know what we mean when we talk about "the moving of the Holy Spirit among the congregation that night"…but what is a non-believer hearing and understanding in that phrase? How about, "Praying through my problem," or "As people come forward during the invitation." If you are not well-versed in the language of Churchese, then those sentences can be much like listening to a doctor from India with a heavy accent, talking about strokes. Pure gobbledeegook.

I believe God wants His believers to speak simply and clearly, in words anyone can grasp. The Bible says, "Let your yea be yea, and your nay be nay." In our modern language this means to be honest, truthful and forthright. And I believe that also includes 'understandable.' Paul wrote, "I can speak in a variety of languages, but I'd rather speak a few words that men understand, that they may hear the gospel."

What are we saying, and how are we saying it? Do people grasp what we are talking about, or are we wasting our breath and their time? God made the Gospel simple enough that little children can "get it." We should never make the mistake of making it difficult. Remember to slow down, interpret for them the phrases you and I take for granted, and make certain that they understand God's wonderful plan.

VII

INTEGRITY: IT AIN'T ALWAYS EASY

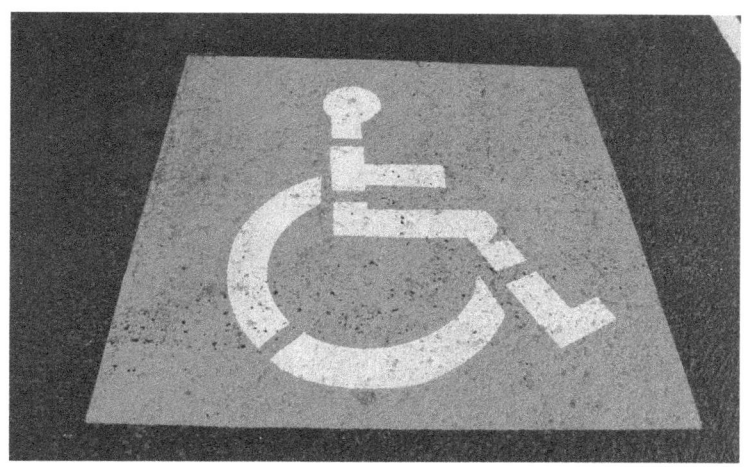

STAND YOUR GROUND, SWEET LADY

Mrs. Average turned into the crowded parking lot of her local department store and finally found a parking space. After locking her car door, she headed rapidly toward the entrance, intent on finishing up quickly and beating the crowds back onto the congested highways. Like everyone else that day, she had things to do and places to be, with not nearly enough time to get it all done.

But as she neared the section for Handicapped Parking, she watched a sleek, black, powerful late-model sports car whip into one of the nearby spaces reserved for the handicapped. Who would have a physical problem with walking, and be behind the wheel of such a beautiful and active-minded vehicle? Fascinated with the possibilities, she deliberately slowed down and watched to see who exited.

Out of the vehicle jumped a man. Not just any male. An extremely fit-looking, heavily muscled athletic man who looked to be in his late thirties. With absolutely no sign of a physical struggle in getting out, shrugging into his expensive-looking jacket or striding around the back of his sports car.

She stood stock-still in amazement. Glancing down, she saw no handicapped sticker on his license plate. Bending slightly, she glanced into his car to see if there might be a handicapped placard hanging from the mirror on the dash. Nada. By then the man had noticed her standing mid-lane, staring at him and his car. He gave her a quick polite nod of the head and started past her.

At that point, something inside of her snapped. Ignoring her normal tendency to 'just-let-it-be-it's-simply-not-worth-it,' she stepped forward and stopped him with a request to ask him this question. "Why did you park in a Handicapped Only space, with no sticker in sight on your car?" With a quick glance at the parking sign, he shrugged and then arrogantly told her, "Ah, it's all right, I'm just gonna be a few minutes."

A short conversation ensued, regarding the need of keeping those spaces for those actually handicapped. The man refused to change his viewpoint, so she wisely gave up. Instead, she reached into her bag for her phone, and began photographing him standing near his license plate and the large Handicapped Only sign in front of his car.

"What are you doing?"

"Getting pictures so I can report this car to the store manager and to the police."

Glaring resentfully at her and mumbling, "@#)$%^&$, FINE!!" he then jumped into his car and with tires squealing, raced away presumably to find another parking spot.

No loud angry public spectacle, no rudeness, and no violence. Just one woman, quietly standing her ground based on her convictions. The Bible says to not be hateful, but to "stand, and then stand again," when confronted with things that are obviously wrong.

Never ignore injustice, but don't lose your cool and act a fool, in order to make your point.

NO LAWYERS OR COURTS NEEDED ON THEIR LAND

"C'mon, Daisy, ya' ain't sick, and ya' shore 'nuff ain't old, so jest keep movin'."

Dan Durbin urged his beloved dappled gray mare up the gently sloping land and halted near a huge sycamore. Waited in the cold gray dawn for his neighbor to show up for their prearranged meeting. This early-morning 'springtime cowboy conference' had been going on for six years, ever since Earl Jackson bought the small ranch on the west side of Dan's modest spread.

Years ago, the two owners had agreed to share the grazing land that lay between them. Now it was time once again to make plans for the annual round up. But they knew there was no need for the same ground to be covered by both ranches. They would simply divide the land between their men, who would bring in all the cattle they found. Then the cattle would be separated, according to the brand found on their hips. An unbranded baby calf born that winter would stick close to its momma, and both would then be delivered to their rightful owner.

Earl broke the peaceful silence with his cheerful "Mawnin' there, Mistah

Durbin" as he pulled his own horse up to stand beside Dan's.

"Waal, look who decided ta' sleep until plumb middle of th' day, like a little lady a' leisure" was the reply.

"Huh! I sho' 'nuff may be a little late for this heah meetin', but my horse stalls done been mucked out. How 'bout at yore place? Betcha that ol' rooster of yore's don't even bother wakin' up til' 'bout noon."

The good-natured insults continued for a few minutes, then Dan brought up the reason they were meeting.

"So. Which part of th' range ya' want yore little pansie-boys to ride this year, Earl?"

Earl spit out the ever-present toothpick he had in his mouth, "Pansies?!" Tell ya' what, my 'pansies' will take th' north half, with all those canyons to search thru. Let you and yore tenderfoots have th' south, where it's smooth 'n simple ridin' thru those trees. Ya' jest mite git halfway done 'bout th' time we're a'sittin' down to supper!"

But finally, the last abusive remark was flung and the search boundaries were set and understood. Then the direct and unflinching gaze of both men met, as strong hands simultaneously reached out for a firm handshake.

Their successful sharing of grazing land and returning mommas and babies to the rightful owner relied solely upon trust and integrity. Trust that each would be honest. And both would have the integrity to keep only what belonged to his ranch.

No lawyers haggling over written contracts. No court needed to force a neighbor to obey the law. Just two men with integrity before God. A solid handshake and a direct stare into the eyes of his neighbor. Both men believing the other would do just what he said he would do.

That handshake was a binding contract.

BETTER CHECK YOUR FLY, PREACHER

A goodhearted momma once approached her well-known and popular pastor after he had completed a stirring message that Sunday morning. She politely introduced herself and then told him, "My son is studying to be a minister at So-and-So Seminary nearby. What is a good piece of advice that you would give him about preparing to preach?" The older and very experienced minister hesitated and with a smile, he looked down into her earnest face and said, "Madam, I would advise him that before he steps into the pulpit, always check his fly!"

Can't you imagine the look of surprise and embarrassment on that sweet little lady's face? She was anticipating some great earth-shaking piece of wisdom, and instead received a tongue-in-cheek bit of advice. But from one who had been there many times and learned a thing or two.

A lot of people seem to be looking for the grandiose in life – when just a few simple and practical truths would serve much better. Why? Because if we don't take care of the small details in our life - the tiny mundane things that prepare us for bigger things - the world may never see the plans and ideas we have in mind.

Benjamin Franklin once said, "Take care of the pennies, and the dollars take care of themselves." He is saying that if you ignore the insignificant, you can create major damage to what you are trying to accomplish. (Can you imagine trying to listen to a preacher who has accidentally left his fly open?)

We knew a young minister who was so determined to make his mark on the world. He had tremendous passion and a burning desire to make a difference for Jesus – but he had ignored the need for formal training or education. After a few years of experiencing a lot of heartache and very limited success, he made an appointment with a well-known pastor and presented his problem to him.

The older gentleman listened intently and ask questions, then told the young man, "God can use any ol' axe to do His work, but He can use a sharpened axe much easier and faster. You need to go back to school and finish your education."

The young man wisely took his advice and years later finally received his doctorate in ministry. No doubt about it, his work after his education definitely had a deeper and wider quality, with more long-lasting effects.

Life is made up of so many so-called insignificant details. And they can seem irritatingly vague and boring as you have to work through them every day. But remember, rarely do the "big events" in life just happen by themselves. They are the result of taking care of those tiny boring details of daily life, which prepare a person for the center-stage God has planned for him.

Don't make the mistake of turning your nose up at the daily details of life, and living only for the Big Stuff. Like the lady said, "Well-tended pennies can turn into dollars, but untended dreams can turn into fluff."

B.O.L.O. FOR THESE PEOPLE

Andy has always liked a good police drama. All the way back to the vintage days of Adam 12, Dragnet, and up to the current series, Blue Bloods. Yes, I can hear the shocked amazement, but he is that old (and so are many of you, but you won't own up to it.)

Anyway, through the years, some of the police vernacular and acronyms have stuck with him. Phrases like "APB" – all points bulletin; "10-20" – going to lunch; and "LEO" – law enforcement officer. Or "B.O.L.O." – be on the lookout.

No doubt about it. We need some special BOLOs today.

Like People of True Character. Find and surround yourself with those who build you up, rather than pull you down. Remember the phrase, "Show me your friends and I'll show you your future." Be aware of the company you keep, because the people around you have a very real and certain influence upon your life. Proverbs 4:14-15 says, "Enter not in the way of evil men; avoid it, pass by it; turn from it."

Another BOLO? Chances to Help Ourselves. Laziness and indifference is decried throughout the Bible. Why? Because those two personal traits bring on problems in life, and life has enough problems on its own. Proverbs 6:6-8 tells us that we need to learn from the ant how to work and provide for ourselves. Paul wrote, "If a man will not work, he does not eat."Hmmmm ...pretty strong stuff in this day and age of the prevailing attitude that, "Society owes me and needs to help me."

We also need a BOLO out for Opportunities to Help Others who truly need our help. Jesus taught that we are to be aware of others' needs and be willing and eager to help when we can. Generally speaking, people who are consumed with only their own needs and desires seem to wind up being lonely and bitter folks. True stuff, folks, finding ways to bless others brings blessing upon yourself.

And we need People Who Will Stand For What is Right. Anybody can be caught up in the flowing current of popular behavior, but a real man stands steady and strong against what is just simply wrong. Ever tried to keep your feet under you and stand steady in a swiftly flowing stream of water? If you have, then you know that it takes strength, a real sense of balance, focus, and determination to stand securely with all that pressure coming at you and trying to knock you off center. It takes a real man or woman to stand up for what they believe.

One more. Find Opportunities and Ways to Talk About Jesus. He told us, "As you go, teach others about Me." Believers need to find ways to share Jesus with anyone, anyway, and any time. If you love the person you are talking to, find a way to insert the love and goodness of Jesus into the conversation.

By the way, centuries ago God himself issued a longstanding BOLO, "TWHMMY" - Those Who Haven't Met Me Yet.

FACEBOOK SHOULDN'T BE A DIRTY LAUNDRY BIN

Saw a quote recently that needs to be read by more people: "There are only two decent places for dirty laundry; the clothes hamper and the washing machine."

Very accurate.

Seems social media is the favorite place for some folks to air their dirty laundry. Personal problems, relationship abuse, and anger issues are fair game out there. Too many who have access to Facebook, a grievance and two fingers that can type, just feel free to "Let'r fly, boys!" and give their whole online world access to any private problems, thoughts and emotions.

Not saying to deny what you are feeling. On the contrary, your emotions are yours and they're not good or bad – they just are. And not saying that what you are going through is just tiny stuff – there is way too much pain and evil out there for anyone to say that. But think about this. Once you put it out on social media, IT'S PUBLIC KNOWLEDGE. And if what you wrote is about an issue that gets resolved, put behind you, and you would prefer it to stay that way – guess what? That ain't happening!

You may prefer to never hear about it again, but now you won't have a choice in the matter. Anyone who saw it on FB may feel free to try to discuss it with you, (or with countless others…ever heard of the good ole Gossip Mill?) You can easily be The Topic for brutal chatter behind your back for a long time.

Be honest with yourself. Your reason for trashing someone on social media is to get your message out there, "I am right and the other person is wrong, and I want everyone to know it." And if the other person does the same, then both of you have dirty undies hanging on the line, with everyone watching them wave in the wind. Dirty laundry is never pretty and believe me, it will be associated with your name for a long time.

Another reason to resist posting your problem on social media; you are going to get skewed feedback.

Scripture states that we are to seek reconciliation as much as possible. That becomes a lot more difficult when you have invited every online Tommy, Dick and Harriet to side with you and tell you how badly you have been offended. And you are going to have a lot harder time seeing the situation honestly when they are telling you that you are not to blame in any way. Really? You are innocent of any wrong-doing in your situation? Then you are the one person on earth other than Jesus, to ever accomplish that one.

Folks, you are much better off to seek the counsel of someone who only wants to help both of you see the truth. It's a mighty thin pancake that only has one side.

Face the truth honestly; you have played a part in this struggle, and a bit of the dirty laundry hanging out there is yours.

A HUGE SALUTE TO ALL THE CARETAKERS OUT THERE

When he was a pastor, Andy was confronted many times with just how unloving and uncaring some folks can be. He was continuously shocked by the brutal way people treat each other today. And then he was shocked that he could still be shocked.

But one day, there came a refreshing break from all the callousness.

While sitting in the waiting area, waiting for his own cancer treatment one day, he began talking to a woman in her mid-thirties who had brought a young child into that same medical facility. During the conversation she told him that the sad-faced little girl sitting so quietly next to her had cancer. She was not only receiving treatment at that hospital, but also at two other facilities. All at the same time. Diagnosed about six months ago, this child had already spent weeks in the hospital, enduring chemotherapy, radiation, and other medical procedures.

As he sat watching this little one, the sparkling energy of a typical seven-year-old was missing. There was only the listlessness of severe illness in her movements. Her pale little face had a tube in her nose, and a brightly colored knit cap covered her sleek head.

As he continued talking with the woman, he sympathetically mentioned her little daughter. She quickly replied, "Oh, no sir, she isn't my daughter. She's my niece. I only got her four months ago. Her dad isn't anywhere to be found, and her mom...well, she's in jail for drugs."

He then remarked to the aunt that what she was doing was admirable – stepping in and taking care of the child in place of the parents. She admitted that it was very hard, added to the responsibility of her own children, and also having to keep her full-time job. But she had known someone had to do it, and so she did.

Andy's heart faltered as he gazed at the child. So many emotions ran through him all at the same time. Pity for the aunt, brokenhearted for the girl, and deep anger at her parents. A dad who just simply walked away and a mom who put drugs before her own tiny child.

Choices.

Those parents decided to put other things in their lives before their own helpless little one. She had been abandoned by the two people who should have loved her and been there for her at all costs.

But she had an aunt. Someone who made the choice to sacrifice her own needs. To be there for this little girl. Someone who chose to accept responsibility for her when others refused. Someone who decided to love her and care for her, no matter what. This little girl needed a 'someone,' and that someone stepped forward.

If God places a situation in front of you, and you feel that certain something that urges you to be a 'someone,' what will you do? Better question; what would any of us do?

Day after day in that treatment center, Andy watched the ongoing results in the body language of that aunt taking on the responsibilities for her desperately ill niece. He saw the exhaustion on her face and the tension in her body as she brought the child for treatment each day. There was no doubt how it cost her. Physically, emotionally and financially. But what she was doing was loyal, brave, and praiseworthy.

Being a 'someone' isn't fun or comfortable or easy, but it is so needed. We stand in deep respect and honor for all the 'someones' out there in this world. You are doing a wonderful thing and we admire you greatly.

LOOKING FOR A HUGE DUMPSTER

Recently our son, who is a pastor, recorded a holiday video at the request of a Phoenix news outlet. The question given to him to address; "What would you give America for Christmas?" Brian's answer to that question? He stated that he would like to give America one huge dumpster. A place to deposit their negativity and pain, so they could go on and live their life without all the baggage. Good answer.

First of all, wouldn't it be wonderful if people could somehow do away with their anger and hostility? We see and hear it everywhere – from the common man's house to the White House. Folks seem angry with everyone and with everything...price of food, government representatives, football polls and border walls.

But while we are ditching stuff, let's add in our prejudices against those not like us. Those whose beliefs do not coincide with ours. Those who hold tightly to their way of life, just as we hold to ours.

People somehow believe the other person has to be wrong, if they do not smell, behave, and think like them. But folks, being different doesn't make anyone automatically wrong. If an American moves to a foreign country, in that country the American's ways will certainly fall into the category of "different." But does that mean he is wrong? No, he just probably has some 'splainin' to do to his new neighbors. As they probably have never been confronted with his way of doing things before. Hopefully no resentment or grudges over the differences will be held.

But why are we holding grudges at all? We live in the "great melting pot" of nationalities. Each one has brought their creative ideas and genius to our nation, and that in itself is an enormous part of our nation's strength. And even beyond that reasoning, the Bible teaches that we all came from the same blood, therefore we are brothers and sisters. We need to practice love and patience with our relatives.

Another thing that could end up in the dumpster - why not toss out the sense of entitlement that is so prevalent today? You know…people who think they deserve something given to them. Who do not see the reason to work for what they want. They somehow believe that "Everyone who has more than me should have to share with me, and someone should be responsible for taking care of me." This is a deadly way of thinking. It leads its victim into remaining trapped, emotionally and financially, always having to lean on someone else.

Another thought on using that huge dumpster; let's dump unforgiveness! When you refuse to forgive and let go of hurtful memories, you have to carry that heavy load around with you. A wise man once said, "He who seeks revenge must be willing to dig two graves. One for the offender and one for himself." Unforgiveness can settle into angry bitterness, and bitterness left unchecked can harden into depression.

God says to forgive and be forgiven. To not let the sun set on your anger. He said that for your sake, not for the one who offended you.

Yep, a humongous dumpster would be a good idea.

IF NOTHING ELSE, SALUTE THE UNIFORM

Andy was once approached by two of his church members, military men, who asked him to become an Army chaplain. As such, his military rank would have required them to salute him. In amusement, he mentioned that fact. Their laughing response? "Remember, Pastor, we are required to salute the uniform, not the man who wears it!"

Are you one of the United States of America citizens who have, or have had, trouble holding your nation's leaders up in respect? You feel they have let you down by conducting their authority badly? You listened to their speeches and have found yourself increasingly disappointed and shocked at how the job is/was handled, versus what was promised. As I'm sure you know, you are not the first to feel this way.

Throughout the years since the birth of our beloved country, people have used their democratic right to vote as they see fit. "I believe that dude will help lead this country the way I think it should go, so yep, I'm gonna vote for that 'un right thar!"

Then, lo and behold! That politician let you down. Whether it was because of- ummm- financial persuasions, (No, say it ain't so!") a change in their beliefs because the wind shifted, or maybe you have had to hear that person loftily declare, "You people simply have not comprehended the complexity of the issues at hand."

Whatever the cause, you got stuck with that person in charge, and you detest where they are leading. In your opinion, some people wear the weight of responsibility and authority well, and conduct themselves with honesty, compassion, and wisdom. Others…well, not so much.

But whether you or I admire the way a person is doing their job, or absolutely detest it, there is one basic truth that we must apply. It is this; you do not have to salute the PERSON in the office, but remember, it is imperative that the OFFICE itself be held in respect.

Why? Because when we as a nation lessen our respect for the authority of the office itself - simply put, we lose. A people who has decided it is acceptable to hold contempt for their nation's authoritative offices will too soon find itself spiraling downward. Abe Lincoln is quoted, "A nation divided against itself cannot stand."

The answer to disagreeing with leadership in our country lies in prayer for guidance, and then lawful action under direction of the Great Authority Himself, God Almighty. In Romans 13:1, the Holy Word of God says, "Let every soul be subject unto the higher powers. For there is no power but of God; the powers that be are ordained of God."

Remember to respect the office. Pray for the one holding that office. Use lawful action under the direction of God Himself.

Like Andy's friends told him; "We are required to salute the uniform - just not necessarily the person wearing that uniform."

VIII

WE'RE ALL A MESS: BUT GOD'S FIXING THAT

BUT... PLEASE DOC, NOT MY COFFEE!

As any of you who know Andy can well remember, he enjoys his coffee. Morning, afternoon, or evening, or with any meal you can name, he has been known to slurp down a cup or two.

So imagine his dismay when a few years ago, an oncologist banned his coffee intake for a few months. Along with a few other foods that he loves and regularly scarfs. Yes, he realized that it was only for a short time. And he knew that it was for his own good…for his health. And he willingly gave up all the other banned food items, in order for the treatments to work.

"But…my coffee?! That's goin' a little too far, don'cha think, Doc?"

But then the good doctor explained to him why there was no choice, so Andy began to persuade myself, "Okay, I can do this. Piece of cake. I just have to be strong. Nothing should be in control of me, except my God, so I got this!"

Sigh…a few days later when he walked into the medical facility for his first treatment, he was struck full in the face by the pungent, sweet aroma of hot coffee! Yes, he knew full well that he shouldn't even go anywhere near that area, but it was irresistible, and he followed his nose to the facility's break room.

Where he saw an intoxicating array of coffee selections displayed beside a very expensive and unique-looking coffee maker.

He was transfixed, paralyzed by the sight of people sipping on a cup of hot fragrant coffee. And he had to just stand there and inhale. And yes, he later admitted it. The green-eyed monster took over, and he had to deal with jealousy, resentment and a certain amount of self-pity.

All of that to say this; we all are drawn to things we cannot have. Whether it be physical, financial, emotional or spiritual, the self-absorbed human being that we all are wants what it wants. And most of them are things that are enticing and unattainable.

Sin has a special appeal, as Satan tries every possible means to attract and draw us away from what God wants for us. But God is just like Andy's oncologist, who for his sake had banned coffee while he was under treatment for cancer. The only times God deliberately tells us "No" are to the things that He knows will not be good for us.

He is a perfect God and a good God, and His motivation is to guide and protect us from harm. God is not seeking to limit your enjoyment of life. On the contrary, He wants to protect you from harm, so that you CAN enjoy the life given to you.

DOES THE ALMIGHTY CREATOR EVER MAKE MISTAKES?

Tough one.

When you think of babies born without arms or legs. You witness hardened criminals allowed to go scot-free, over and over again. A war perpetrated against a country who has not committed such crimes that would warrant that action. People drawn into drug addiction that they can't break. When you hear the new reports that so many helpless young girls have been sold into sex slavery. Watch as a heartless powerful dictator is living high, while his countrymen are suffering in starvation and poverty. When you read of, or are personally acquainted with, a person who feels that they are trapped in the body of the wrong sex.

Throughout time, some have held the belief that God the Creator has made mistakes in allowing things like this to happen.

Well, first of all, if God, the creator of everything has made a mistake, I sure wouldn't want to be the one created being that has the guts to stand up and tell The All-Powerful One that He did! I may not be the most intelligent, but I do have more brains than that.

Secondly, yes, definitely we are surrounded by heartbreaking circumstances everywhere we look. Absolutely no doubt about that. But, is that reality a result of God's inattention, His vengefulness, His uncaring? Or rather, is it a result of sin – the behavior that God Himself has warned men and women against throughout all generations of time?

The Bible is filled with cautions and pleadings from Him, telling people what the inevitable result of sin will be. Pain and heartache. And remember, the consequences of bad behavior are not visited just on the person who acted against God's advice. We are all interconnected, and therefore what I do affects you and yours.

Little children suffer badly from the decisions made in the generations before them. Innocent people are terribly hurt when someone decides they can do anything they so please – regardless of God's warnings against sinning.

I have heard the statements, "Well, good grief, He is God! He could stop all this pain and suffering with a blink of His eye if He wanted to. So why doesn't He, if He is a loving God?

Yep, He certainly could.

Except for one thing. Seems our loving God doesn't believe in forcing anyone to act right. That would make us no more than human puppets, and He doesn't appear to want that for us. He evidently has placed limits on His power to make us do what is good and right.

Our God allows us to live in sin if that is what we choose. But why would He do that? Couple of reasons. He wants us to obey Him, not out of fear and oppression, but from love. And also, because He deliberately didn't create us as robots, unable to think, reason, and have affection.

When you look honestly at the facts, we humans are the reason there is so much pain in this world, not God.

WHO ARE YOU ROOTING FOR?

Probably most everyone has a favorite college team that we like to support. If you love sports, that is. Here in the state of Oklahoma, some people are serious followers of the Sooners, others are avid Cowboy fans. And there are countless other college teams that have the devoted loyalty of their fans. This leads to competition that is not just confined to the players, but also among the supporters. This rivalry is natural and if kept in proper perspective, it is healthy and fun.

There are always debates, teasing and even ridicule among fans over the various strengths and weaknesses of their particular teams. But even if the debate becomes radical and heated, our agreement or disagreements do not cause serious eternal consequences. In other words, it isn't a life-or-death matter. (Though if you listen to some fans, you would almost come to believe that their team winning The Championship this year actually is that crucial.)

But there is whole 'nother issue, another enormous struggle, and it is for The Real Championship. And it does have serious eternal consequences. It is the competition between God and Satan for your eternal soul…deciding where you will spend eternity.

It surrounds your answer to the basic question, "What shall I do then with Jesus?" (Matt. 27:22) This was the question posed many centuries ago. And this is the same question people have to struggle with today. All these centuries later, and it still has be answered by everyone of us.

In John 14:6 Jesus explained, "I am the way, the truth, and the life. No one gets to the Father, except by Me." This means that there is absolutely no way to escape having to answer the question, "What will I do with Jesus?" Everyone who lives on this earth will, at some point, have to face our Sovereign God. And when we do, we will be judged according to our response.

Will you become a staunch follower and cheer Him on? Or maybe you have decided to support another philosophy or belief, and root for a different "team" altogether. Or will you try to just be neutral and not cheer or live for any belief? Just simply adopt the lifestyle of "I live only for today, 'cause I don't believe in no stupid afterlife anyway."

Jesus asked the disciples in John 6, when many supporters had deserted Him, "Will you also go away?" To which Simon Peter replied, "To whom shall we go? Thou hast the words of life." So very true, Peter. There is absolutely no avoiding the One who created us and gives us each breath every day we are alive.

Each of us will face Him at the end, and live the consequences of our answer. Think long and hard about this before you make a decision.

PAPA ONLY WANTED THE BEST FOR HER

His adult granddaughter texted Pappa about her boyfriend. Suzanne told him all about Mr. Wonderful. How excited she was for him and her Nanna to meet this hairy-legged hormone hurricane. She told him about their talks of "future plans" together. Being the sweet level-headed man that he was, of course, Pappa wrote back to her.

Hmmmm, this could be the very first clue that all did not go well.

A few days later, with a very innocent expression on his face, he defensively told her dad, "I promise you, ALL that I said was, "Even at this distance from Shaneekah, California to Wampas, Minnesota, I can already tell you, he's not good enough for you." To which his exasperated son said, "Pappa, there may be a slight communication issue between you guys in the future. Although I can already foresee it will not ever be on your part, of course."

Why would this Pappa risk saying something so obviously divisive? Because he loved his granddaughter. And he was just a wee bit biased. She was his first, and she was very special in his eyes. So, he decided to take the opportunity to make his feelings known on the subject. But he also had an ulterior motive. He wanted to cause her to think about who she is, and the kind of young husband she deserves.

Honestly, there were many fine (and many not-so-fine) young men out there that she could have been attracted to, and any one of them could have fallen in love with her and married Suzanne. And that couple could have had a relationship that would "work." But Pappa didn't want a marriage for his princess that would just "work." He dreaded seeing her just settle for a relationship that would be okay. He wanted his granddaughter to make certain this man was God's very best for her.

God must feel the same way about His children. "Just wait for me to give you what is best for you, child."

You see, God looks into our lives and sees what are good ideas and plans... to our way of thinking. We strategize, and we plot our course and we actually believe we have made some great decisions. We may even desire and ask Him for His approval and blessing on our plans. But the God of Creation can look into your present situation and your future, and declare with complete authority, "That's not good enough for you, I have planned something so much better for your life."

The Bible tells us that God does indeed have good plans for us, things to bless and prosper our lives. (Jeremiah 29:11) He is not a kill-joy, just the exact opposite. He is a concerned Heavenly Father who greatly loves His children. He wants the very best for all of them – whether we realize it or not.

End of the story about the out-spoken Pappa? He finally grudgingly admitted to his son, "Yeah, I guess 1 do need to wait and meet this ugly Neanderthal before I pass judgment. But I only want the best for my little darlin'. And I still reserve the right as her Pappa to despise him."

Pappas....ya' just gotta love'em.

DRINK, PEOPLE, DRINK!

While we were away from home for a few days, in our absence the potted plants on our back deck had started to wilt badly from lack of water. Oops, flat forgot to make arrangements for them. Some of them were close to going ten toes up, and you know what I mean. So, I gave them all a good long soaking drink of water and watched as they all seemed to sigh a collective "Ahhh!"

Within a very short amount of time those poor withered plants had rebounded, and once again stood straight and tall. What a huge difference a little water made! They went from being shrunken and dry to vibrantly healthy and full of life.

It was so similar to watching believers living their Christians lives. If they are not tended and "watered" regularly, they seem to wither, dry up and become nearly lifeless. But there is a vast difference between plants and Christians. The big difference? Plants never voluntarily starve themselves of the water they need. It is only through a drought or from the plant owner's neglect that plants end up in such sad shape.

But Christians? For some reason, we willingly and knowingly withdraw from the Source of the very Water we need. And the dustier we are, the more we want to be left alone. There seems to be varied reasons for us turning our back on Him; too busy with life, hurt feelings from an incident at church, or maybe the pride gets bruised. But the result seems to be much the same – withdrawing from the Healer and Life-giver who can help.

Dropping out of church, neglecting to read the Bible and ignoring any prayer time with our God is the typical pattern. Oh yes, life will seem to continue on with very little apparent change – at first. But before long the people around you, who know you on a daily basis, can sense something is definitely wrong. And if left in this circumstance for very long, that poor Christian will end up in a severe state of pain.

Am I saying Christians are completely hopeless after hitting this wilted condition? No, of course not. But they are feeling the emotional dryness and spiritual weakness that comes with it. And life will have lost some of its joy. Hurts that they used to easily overlook and forgive will stay with them. Work and play that once seemed so important to them will lose some of the luster they once knew.

It's simply not worth it, but yet we all sink into that condition at one time or another.

Get determined to find whatever it was that happened to you to bring on this dry period in your life. Sit down, let yourself feel, and follow your thoughts all the way to the root of your problem. Then do what you need to do...for your sake.

Jesus said, "Come unto me all who are weak and heavy-laden, and I will give you rest." A Christian can always return to Christ for His care and blessing.

FATHER ISN'T NECESSARILY SPELLED F-A-T-H-E-R

You can spell it D-a-d, or D-a-d-d-y, F-a-t-h-e-r or P-o-p, or many other variations. But you are talking about the dominant male role model in a person's life. The person who helped create who you have become. Let me give you some other variations of the spelling, which help to showcase that man's real role.

How about P-R-E-S-E-N-T? According to 2021 U.S Census Bureau, of the about eleven million single parent households with children under the age of eighteen, nearly eighty eight per cent are led by women. So many of our male parents are invisible to their children. They are simply nowhere around.

It is nearly impossible to effectively parent a child from a distance, and complete absence from their life is even worse. The negative effect on a child whose dad is not in their life on a consistent basis, in a positive, loving, authoritative way, is being well documented by the disastrous results of these last years. When are these absent fathers going to man up, step up, and stick around?

Another way to spell Father is L-O-V-E. And don't start up with the old tired line that your affection is shown by putting "a roof over their head and biscuits on the table." A paycheck will never replace a man with a gentle touch, a kind encouraging word, firm discipline, and a positive example.

How about we spell Father in another way... S-E-C-U-R-I-T-Y. Part of the male responsibility is to protect and make his family feel secure. Feeling secure is an emotion, and just sending money to support them - while you live somewhere else doing your own thing - does not provide emotional security to your family. It is the God-given job of a father to let his children know that they are vitally important, and will always be important to him. And simply saying those words to them on the phone never conveys to them what they are needing. You.

R-O-L-E M-O-D-E-L is another way to spell Father. The Bible teaches that men are to show their children how to live – to let the child actually see and hear how you deal with everyday life. Talk is cheap, guys. But being a role model who actually lives daily life as a real man in front of his family? That is priceless.

How does a young boy grow up to know how he is to live life as a man? He watches the males that surround him, of course. By imitating his boyhood role model – good or bad. And how do young girls select what kind of boy to date and eventually marry? How do they sense what kind of treatment they should expect from their future husband? Much of the time, a young lady will select a mate that subconsciously reminds her of the dominant male role model in her childhood. Guys, that means she will most likely marry a guy with your emotional weaknesses. Ouch.

Now, all that is some pretty stiff info to chew on. So let me change the tone a little bit.

Congratulations to all you loving dads, step-dads, and stand-in dads out there. You love your kids well, provide constant emotional security, and are truly present in their lives. You have been given an awesome and difficult task in life and the world admires a great dad. And to the rest, who are struggling but really are trying to get it right? Find a mentor, ask your Heavenly Father for help, and be open with your family about your weaknesses. And the ones who have just deliberately walked away? You know what you need to do.

GOD ISN'T TRYING TO SPOIL YOUR FUN

Our oldest son at fifteen months old was toddling around, jabbering constantly, and always adventurous - ready to experience this world for himself. Knowing this rather daring streak in him, we tried to keep him in sight of one of us at all times. But the day came when both of us thought the other had him, so Brian was "free-ranging" in the parsonage that our church pastorate provided.

Finally we realized that neither of us had the baby, so the frantic search began. Didn't take long in that small house to recognize that he was not in any room, so we quickly expanded our search to outside. Sure enough, there he was, on the front porch.

At first a parent only feels relieved and grateful to find their child, but on the heel of those emotions comes, "How in the world did he figure out how to undo the lock and open that door?"

The front porch of that old farmhouse was about four feet off the ground, and had no safety railing of any kind around it, just a porch and a set of concrete steps that led down to the lawn. Andy opened the door and walked out to grab him away from the possible danger. But then he also saw the large, calm, and friendly dog that had wandered up to our house a couple of days before. Obviously someone's pet who had wandered away.

That dog was walking slowly and carefully beside our baby – always with his bulky body on the outside next to the edge of the porch, never letting Brian get near the dangerous drop-off. When Andy saw what was happening, he stopped and simply watched. (Yes, I can hear your gasp of dismay, but it was clear that something very special was happening on that porch that morning.)

Dressed only in a diaper and t-shirt, "Brian, the Ever-Adventurous and Determined One," evidently had decided that since he had successfully escaped the house, he was ready to leave the porch and head out to conquer the world. He had one hand on Fido's back with his tiny fingers wrapped in the dog's long fur, using it to keep his balance as he would toddle toward the concrete steps that led to freedom. But as he would approach that dangerous area, the dog would block his path and nudge him away. So, Brian would turn around and walk back the other way, trying his best to get around that dog.

We quietly watched this play out for the next minute or so, as a determined baby tried to get to danger and an equally determined dog stopped his progress. Brian would get frustrated, whine, pull Fido's fur and hit the back of his protector, but that gentle animal never budged from his post.

This memory from long ago reminds me of God. We sometimes do our darndest to get into mischief or engage in ol' plain rebellion, but then we find that "something" is blocking our path and making life difficult for us. That 'something' is God and He isn't being mean or spiteful. He is simply trying to prevent us from suffering from a certain and painful fall. No matter how we whine and rage at Him, He faithfully stays with us.

Scripture says, "Thou has set before and behind me, and put your hand upon me….Thou art there." (Psalms 139:5 and 8b) God seeks to only protect and do what is best for us. He only tells us 'NO' to things that he knows will hurt us.

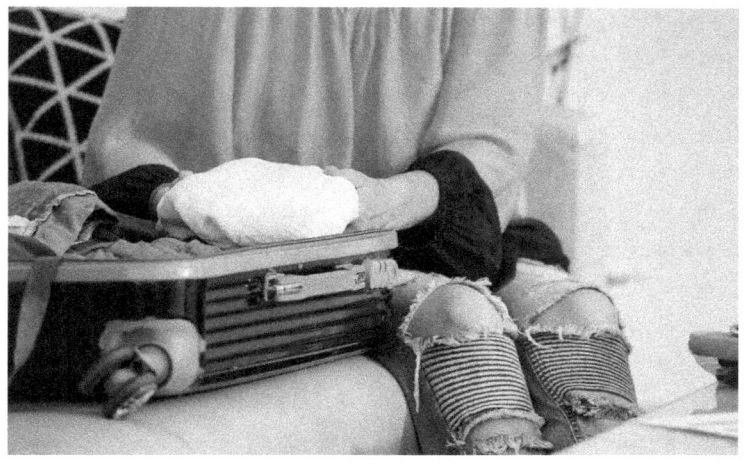

THE MILD-MANNERED AND THE REVENGE SEEKER

Have you ever made an enemy? Someone who not only detests you, but actually would love to see the ground open up and swallow you. While they laugh and annihilate everything that used to be yours.

No? Neither have I. Or at least I hope not. If I have, they haven't let me know it…yet.

But for now, let's just assume that I have made someone very angry. That I have done something so awful in their eyes that this person detests the air that I am allowed to breathe. An act which hurt them deeply enough that they want to destroy me and everything that pertains to me. That's scary. To think that I could be living on borrowed time in someone's daydreams.

What would I do? Probably want to pack my bag and run in the middle of the night, to be perfectly honest. Just escape with my skin still on, with anxiety as my companion. Most likely, it would never occur to me to face my accuser head-on and try to resolve the problem.

And while I am at it, I will also admit, I am not a Get-Evener. Revenge doesn't really live in the gene pool of this lady. But self-preservation? Absolutely. Like I said earlier, pack my bags and hide where I can never be found.

Does that admission make you cringe? Are you a strong, "Take charge, shoot first, and ask questions later," kind of person? Lot of you people out there, I know. People who can't understand someone like me.

But maybe, you are one of those who do understand my emotions, "Very little is worth living in fear and pain. I'd rather start over somewhere else." If you are, accept it. You are who you are, and you are no more wrong - nor right - than the "You Can't Bully Me, I'll Get Revenge" clan.

But there was one man unlike any of us. He made enemies because he knew who he was, and he knew what he believed. And when his enemies attempted to kill him he didn't run, neither did he cave on his stand. But he also never attempted revenge on them. He just stood. And loved. Friend or foe. And he willingly forgave and blessed anyone who changed their mind about him.

Honestly, it would never cross the brain of someone like me to simply stand their ground, while just intensely loving the one who hated me. And it would never cross the mind of a "You Can't Bully Me, I'll Get Revenge" club member either.

Why? Because we are not perfect in our thoughts and our emotions. We are very human.

But Jesus Christ was perfect in His walk on this earth. Oh yes, do not doubt, He experienced every emotion that we humans experience. Fear, temptation, anger, and all the rest. But one humongous difference between Him and us. He was never controlled by those emotions and thoughts.

STINKIN' THINKIN'

The boy sure had learned some choice words, no doubt about it. In the school room, on the playground, and at home, his rather, ummm, colorful way of expressing his thoughts and feelings kept him in trouble on a regular basis. Making it worse, his friends loved to push his buttons, just to make him angry enough to sound off in no uncertain terms.

His parents and teachers at school had corrected, disciplined, and even punished him for using words that would make a sailor feel at home – seemingly to no avail. But gradually, consequences for his behavior began to really hurt. And finally realizing those punishments were only going to get worse, he knew he had to make the effort to hold his tongue. So the work began. Torn between obedience and habit, sometimes he slipped up, but he was honestly trying to reform.

All was going fairly well, until the day 'SHE did it.'

A young tormentor in his classroom, who had gotten bored with his better behavior, decided that she needed to get him into trouble. So, she set about making fun of his appearance, his grades, and even his family.

With every insult, his angry face turned red with the effort to hold his temper, and his hands clenched into little fists while he kicked at the wall nearby. But still, he held out and never said a word. Finally, exasperated at failing to get him to yell words that used to shoot from his lips like fire, she got up in his face and sneered, "Aw, c'mon, aren't you gonna say sumpin' bad?!"

To which he glared and replied through clenched teeth, "Nope, and you can't make me. But if you could hear me thinkin', I'd shore 'nuff get a whuppin'!!

Controlling your thinking and your tongue. Hard to do most of the time. In James 3:8, Scripture says, "But no human being can tame the tongue. It is a restless evil, full of deadly poison."

But even worse, the tongue only obeys what the mind is thinking! No one's tongue just decides to begin flapping on its own. Your thoughts control exactly what comes out of your mouth. Talk about being caught with your pants down!

Stinkin' thinkin' is a real problem for most people. And we don't even realize how hurtful our thoughts are. Try this. Monitor your thoughts. Stop every once in a while, and look back on what has been occupying your mind. Then examine your emotions. If you are like most of us, you have been letting your mind replay heartache, criticism, negativity, or anger. And now you are battling a bad mood or depression.

To quote the writer, James Allen, "Good thoughts bear good fruit, bad thoughts bear bad fruit – and every man is his own gardener."

Stinkin' thinkin' does hurt.

YOU CAN BE A DIFFERENT YOU

When you were a much younger person and much less mature in thoughts and deeds, you probably said and did ill-advised, inconsiderate things. I know I did. But as years passed and I grew wiser, I would look back at my actions and shake my head at my own stupidity.

In all honesty, probably you can say much the same.

Nothing I can now say or do will erase the past mistakes in my life. But I do know this. They are part of my past, and I am not that same person anymore. And the loving people in my life have allowed me the opportunity to mature and change, no longer holding me accountable for the childish actions in my younger years.

But today, things written, said, or done, by any well-known public figure can be held against him or her forever, it seems. People seem to feel that they have the right to demand penalty and payment from public figures for something in their far distant past, even though it is apparent by their lifestyle that they no longer are a person who behaves that way anymore.

This is not an article to declare whether this current tendency is wrong or right. It is just a grateful observation that God does not operate that way!

God sees all and knows all, and yet He has written in His Word that if a person comes to faith in Christ Jesus, that God will forgive everything in that person's past. He removes all shame and guilt that comes with our wrongdoing. And not only does He do that for us, but He also promises to never remember our sin, or ever bring it back up again to us.

Now, let me clarify what I am saying. There are earthly consequences for wrongdoing. That is a truth that cannot be altered. But I am writing about eternal consequences – after your death, are your sins going to be on your shoulders, or are they going to rest on the shoulders of Jesus?

Through His death on that cross, God can and will, delete your deepest, darkest sins. If you realize you are a sinner and believe in Jesus Christ as your Savior, God has promised to lay your sins on Jesus. Jesus' death will pay the debt for what you have done in your life, and you will never be held accountable to God for those sins. Yes, He will expect you to try to live your life from that point to please Him, but He also says that you will not ever be alone in your struggle to live your life. He promises to be with you and to help you.

We humans like to hold grudges, accuse, and hold debts over one another. God never holds grudges against the person who has trusted Jesus and is trying to live his life to please Him. In fact, Scripture says, "As far as East is from the West, so far has He removed our transgressions." Why did He say that? Because East and West never meet. This means that a believer's sins are totally gone, because you can head east as long as you wish, and you will never find yourself headed west.

We're All a Mess, But God's Fixing That

CONCLUSION

Dear reader, thank you for sticking with us to the very end of this book. We hope you have enjoyed the journey, as much as we have had the pleasure of being your tour guides.

Our purpose, hope, and focus for this compilation of CoffeeTime With Andy & Renie articles was not simply for providing a time to sit with a cup of your favorite drink in your hand. While you relax and read something wholesome. Although I do hope that did occur.

Our entire intention and focus was to tell you that God is real. That God is entirely good, all the time. That God only wants the best for all of us. And He never, and I do mean never, quits endeavoring to bring His children into a closer image of Himself in their behavior, emotions and thoughts.

Please keep up with our latest articles, podcasts, speaking events and more at www.coffeetimewithandyandrenie.com.

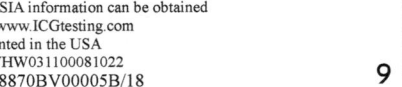 

CPSIA information can be obtained
at www.ICGtesting.com
Printed in the USA
BVHW031100081022
648870BV00005B/18